Research Strategies

for a

Digital Age

Research
Strategies
for a
Digital Age

Bonnie L. Tensen
Seminole Community College

THOMSON

WADSWORTH

United States · Australia · Canada · Mexico · Singapore · Spain · United Kingdom

THOMSON
WADSWORTH

Research Strategies for a Digital Age
Bonnie L. Tensen

Publisher: *Michael Rosenberg*
Acquisitions Editor: *Dickson Musslewhite*
Editorial Assistants: *Stephen Marsi,*
  Marita Sermolins
Senior Production Editor: *Sally Cogliano*
Director of Marketing: *Lisa Kimball*
Executive Marketing Manager: *Carrie Brandon*
Associate Marketing Manager: *Joe Piazza*
Senior Print Buyer: *Mary Beth Hennebury*

Compositor: *WestWords, Inc.*
Project Manager: *Kristin Swanson*
Photography Manager: *Sheri Blaney*
Cover Designer: *Dutton & Sherman*
Text Designer: *Brian Salisbury*
Printer: *Transcontinental*
Cover Photos: © *Comstock Images;*
  S. Wanke/PhotoLink; © *Comstock Images*

For more information contact Wadsworth, 25 Thomson Place, Boston, Massachusetts 02210 USA, or you can visit our Internet site at http://www.wadsworth.com

For permission to use material from this text or product contact us:
Tel   1-800-730-2214
Fax   1-800-730-2215
Web   www.thomsonrights.com

ISBN: 0-1550-5984-X

Library of Congress Control Number: 2003106820

Contents

PART THREE
Research Documentation

Preface

"The Internet is revolutionary, but not Utopian."

ANDREW SHAPIRO ET AL.,
Principles of Technorealism

The enormous impact the Internet has had on the world was underscored by an experience my sister recently had while on vacation in Holmes County, Ohio, in the midst of one of the largest Amish communities in the United States. She needed some information about her next destination, so she made a quick trip to the town's public library. As horse-drawn buggies carrying locals dressed in somber black and gray passed by outside, she discovered an online reference catalog, numerous databases, and access to the World Wide Web inside. Set in the midst of recurring reminders of a slower, less-technological age, this rural library was, nonetheless, completely "wired." Needless to say, she found what she was looking for.

The "information superhighway" has invaded our lives, radically changing the way information is stored and disseminated. Internet technology has transformed the library of the twenty-first century, making *more* information *more* accessible to *more* students. Although no one can dispute that the Internet has greatly increased our access to information, it also creates a special set of problems for students who do not (or cannot) distinguish between the credible sources available via the electronic library and the morass of unregulated information on the World Wide Web. The aim of this book is to teach students

- Basic research strategies and library skills that will enable them to proficiently use online catalogues and databases to locate credible sources in the new, "digital" library
- Researching and evaluative skills that will enable them to identify reliable and academically appropriate information on the World Wide Web
- Proper methods of incorporating and documenting these resources in their research papers

The idea for this text arose from my experiences teaching research and composition in the networked classroom. At first I focused on the use of the electronic tools and neglected the teaching of basic research competencies. When my students handed in their research projects, I began to realize that the two are inextricably intertwined. Given their increased access to information, I expected that they would locate sources that were fair, accurate, *and* scholarly. Instead, their resources tended to be personal Web pages containing biased or unsupported opinion, short newspaper or popular magazine articles that were written by journalists rather than experts, and abstracts of articles (instead of the articles themselves). Many of my students had advanced Internet "surfing" skills, but they lacked research acumen. In the end they were reduced to the scholarly equivalent of "roadkill" on the information superhighway because the sources they located contained inaccurate, incomplete, or misleading information. These experiences convinced me that the traditional must be taught simultaneously with the high tech. Technological ability is now inseparable from information literacy—at least when it comes to writing college papers that require research. *Research Strategies for a Digital Age* emphasizes traditional research strategies and skills in the context of new and emerging technologies.

As a quick glance at the table of contents will show, *Research Strategies for a Digital Age* is divided into three major sections. The first section explains a process for beginning and sustaining a research project. Students are instructed how to use the online library catalog as a starting point to learn (1) the basics of creating *matching terms* and *search phrases* (e.g., keyword and Boolean phrases), (2) the art of research *sleuthing* (the way one scholarly source leads to other valuable resources), and (3) the basics of *source evaluation* (whether a resource is relevant, reliable, and unbiased). The search phrases students develop with the help of the online catalog are then used to explore electronic databases (indices and collections of articles from popular and academic periodicals). This first section of the book contains an extensive and annotated list of databases pertinent to specific academic disciplines and explains the differences between databases that offer only bibliographical information (and/or abstracts) and full-text databases.

The second section of this text teaches students to use these same, time-tested research strategies to cautiously explore the World Wide Web, first, by casting their research nets in "well-stocked ponds" (i.e., search engines, directories, and subject guides) and then by evaluating this information to confirm that it meets the stringent requirements of academic research. The section concludes with a chapter on field research (interviews and surveys) with suggestions about how to maximize their use of the Internet to efficiently conduct these studies.

The final section of *Research Strategies for a Digital Age* begins with a comprehensive warning against plagiarizing. The text describes the "many faces" of plagiarism now made possible by the "cut-and-paste" nature of the World Wide Web and offers examples of improper paraphrasing and summarizing. Also in this section are chapters featuring the most current information on how to document conventional "hard" print sources as well as the new types of electronic resources available. Documentation has become confusing because digital resources are constantly "morphing" into new forms. For instance, databases once exclusively packaged in CD-ROMs are now delivered over the Internet. This text offers the most up-to-date documentation models for the Modern Language Association (MLA), American Psychological Association (APA), Council of Science Editors (CSE), and Chicago Manual of Style (CMS) formats. It includes sample student essays that offer marginal notations to explain the intricacies of in-text and works cited documentation choices.

Research Strategies for a Digital Age is a unique text. There are many "guides to the Internet" available. This is *not* one of them. The ideal starting place for scholarly research has always been, and still is, the academic library; this text teaches students to maximize their use of the new technologies available in our "wired" libraries as well as on the Web. The research paper is a staple of many academic classes, yet most handbooks provide only a cursory explanation of the research process; this text offers a step-by-step progression that enables students to build researching and evaluative skills while introducing them to a variety of research tools. Proper documentation is fundamental to the research project, yet few handbooks or guides provide sufficient examples of the newer forms (e.g., Web sites, database articles) by which information is made available; this text provides an abundance of sample entries of the types of documents students are now using in *four* different styles. Most importantly, *Research Strategies for a Digital Age* is written to appeal to students and actively engage them in the research process. The text features

- Written exercises and assignments so students can practice the skills they have been taught
- Checklist boxes that summarize important information for easy review
- Approximately forty "screen shots" that illustrate the concepts explained in the text
- **E-tips** that explain how students can maximize their use of the computer in the research process
- **Writing Tips** on how to skillfully incorporate direct quotations
- An index to quickly locate information

If a course includes a research component, *Research Strategies for a Digital Age* is the perfect ancillary text that will help students develop research methods and habits (skills that will serve them well throughout their college careers) that are conducive to the "libraries" of today—whether virtual or real.

Acknowledgments

I would like to thank Jane Bradford, "librarian extraordinaire," who first opened my eyes to the benefits of teaching students library skills. In addition, I'm grateful to Julie McBurney for recognizing the usefulness of this project, and for those at Wadsworth—Michael Rosenberg and Sally Cogliano—as well as to Diane Drexler, for their skill and expertise in developing it. I greatly appreciated the excellent suggestions provided by those who thoroughly reviewed the manuscript:

Lara Baker Whelan, *Berry College*
Maryam Barrie, *Washtenaw Community College*
Kathleen McCoy, *Adirondack Community College*

Finally, I would like to thank my friends Nancy Barber and Jane Bolding, who good-naturedly endured and supported me throughout this process (a real friend doesn't look bored, even when you're talking about documentation formats). And I really can't find the words to thank Karen Kaivola for all the help she has given me in writing and in life (but when I do, I'm sure she'll help me edit them for greater clarity and impact).

PART ONE

Research Basics

CHAPTER ONE

Get Off to a Good Start

"The beginning is the most important part of the work."

PLATO, *The Republic*

Perhaps no assignments you receive in college will be more difficult than research papers or projects. After all, for most of your course assignments the instructor will provide the "raw materials" you will need (class readings, lectures, demonstrations, and instructions). But the research project requires that you strike out on your own: You will have to determine a topic, develop an approach that works for you, and base your assertions on reliable information. Finally, after you have expended much effort on these invisible but essential "behind-the-scenes" tasks, you will have to present your findings—accurately, cleverly, persuasively, and intelligently—in an essay, report, or argument. No wonder so many students find the research project difficult!

Establishing a viable topic and locating credible, relevant sources is as challenging and time consuming as it is essential. Because the final written or oral presentation is often the only graded part of the process, some students (foolishly) minimize the amount of effort they expend at the beginning of the process. However, if you have ever tried to write a detailed, informative, and well-supported essay without first focusing and thoroughly researching your topic—without really *knowing* what's important about that topic—you know how difficult it is to sustain anything resembling an intelligent discussion beyond the first paragraph or two. Fortunately, there are tried-and-true methods that can help you get started. This chapter offers strategies for developing a topic that is interesting and researchable.

Step 1: Choose a Topic

Choose a Topic You Care About

Because coming up with a good topic is often a real challenge, some students are most comfortable when instructors assign a specific subject to be researched. They are terrified if they must choose their own. Others chafe at any restrictions and want to determine their own direction. Whichever group you fall into—whether you prefer more structure or greater freedom—the success of your project depends on your active involvement and interest. A research project is hard work, and it is all the more difficult if you don't care about your topic from the start. Even assigned subjects often allow flexibility so you can adapt them to reflect your own particular interests. And although you might feel more comfortable when your instructor specifies the topic, you should never forfeit the opportunity to explore an issue that you are genuinely interested in knowing more about.

Adapt Topics to Your Own Interests

If the subject is assigned, try to shape your approach so that it reflects something that appeals to you, intrigues you, or even annoys you. You should at least experience a spark of curiosity. You should *want* to know more. Ideally, you'll feel much more than a spark of interest, and you'll discover the assignment provides an opportunity for you to learn more about the world, yourself, other people, and/or other cultures. Coming up with this kind of topic is often a matter of learning how to ask good questions.

Discover a Topic You Want to Know More About

Regardless of whether the topic is assigned or you have the freedom to choose your own, make your research project relevant to you.

⏱ *Quick* CHECK

Make Your Project Relevant
Make your project relevant by answering these questions.
- How does this topic relate to any past/present concerns in my life?
- How does this subject relate to issues I have recently been studying or thinking about?
- How might this subject be important to me in the future?
- How can I use this subject to explore something that I want to know more about?

Research is all about finding answers to an intriguing question or a set of questions. A few years ago, one of my students wrote one of the worst research papers I have ever received. It argued that 18-year-olds should be granted the legal right to drink alcohol. The subject is a worthy one (over the years I have received numerous convincing essays that have argued this same point). However, this essay offered no factual evidence or justification and was composed entirely of unsupported (and illogical) conjecture. As I discussed these problems with the student, I realized that he had absolutely no interest in the topic (he had chosen it because he thought *I* would find it interesting). I don't usually allow students to abandon their research projects in the middle of the semester, but I made an exception in this case. In the end, the student produced a meticulously researched essay on methods for conserving the lobster population. His family was in the "lobstering" business, and the diminishing crustacean population threatens their livelihood. Once he discovered a topic he truly cared about, this student's research skills blossomed.

Needless to say, if you are not invested in the topic, you will find it difficult to sustain an attitude that will energize and encourage you throughout the process. That lack of passionate involvement also will be obvious to your readers who will, in turn, feel less interest than they otherwise would. Even if a research assignment seems mind-numbingly uninteresting, you can find a way to transform it into a subject you care about.

Turn a "Boring" Topic into an Interesting One. For example, suppose your American history instructor assigns a research project on "The Effects of the Vietnam War." Your first reaction might be to dismiss this topic as essentially boring—as something that might have appealed to the baby-boomer generation, but not to you. However, unless the professor is very specific about what *types* of effects he/she expects you to study (e.g., the effects of the war on subsequent United States presidential elections), you can find a way to connect the subject with something you really *do* find interesting. If you are majoring in the biological sciences or pursuing a career in a medical field, for instance, you might research the long-term effects of Agent Orange on soldiers who fought in the Vietnam conflict. Someone interested in film or the arts might compare the different ways this war has been represented in film in the decades following the conclusion of American involvement. A sociology major could investigate some of the reasons why popular opinion concerning this war has changed since the 1960s. A student of architecture might consider the factors that influenced the design and construction of the *Vietnam Wall Memorial* in Washington D.C.; it all comes back to knowing yourself and making connections that initially might not seem obvious.

Stumped? Ask Others.   Sometimes answers to questions such as the ones listed earlier might come with virtually no conscious effort on your part. When that happens, the experience can seem almost magical. More often, especially for novice writers, your thinking will seem blocked. You might sit at the computer for hours without accomplishing anything that feels like real progress. That is a perfectly normal (if not particularly pleasant) experience. After all, a research project involves multiple tasks, each of which is complex. At such times it helps to remember that good thinking rarely occurs in a vacuum. If you can't come up with a good topic on your own, seek aid elsewhere.

⏱ *Quick* CHECK

Discover a Topic
Discover a topic you want to know more about.
- *Discuss the project* with your instructor, other students, family, and/or friends.
- *Browse* encyclopedias, newspapers, and the Internet.

Help can come in various forms. One option is to discuss the project with others.

- Make an appointment with your instructor. Explore your interests in conversation and ask for suggestions.
- Discuss the project with an instructor who teaches in your major or minor.

- Talk to other students in the class. After all, they are familiar with the assignment and will probably be eager to bounce ideas off you as well.

- Explain the assignment to friends and family members. Perhaps they can suggest a particular angle on the topic that combines your interests with the assignment.

---

e- TIPS

Using E-mail to Generate Ideas

E-mail is a wonderful way to solicit opinions from others. Some people find it easier to write their questions down than to communicate face-to-face. Also, you might forget a suggestion you hear, but an e-mail response can be printed out. Many instructors include their e-mail addresses on course syllabi. If so, you should feel free to contact them. Exchange e-mail addresses with other students in your class. Sometimes class and work schedules make it difficult to meet to talk, but everybody reads their e-mail. E-mail is also an easy way to connect with people (e.g., family members, friends from home, former teachers) who might be able to offer suggestions.

Talking to someone or writing down your thoughts is a great way to move beyond a mental block. Forcing yourself to articulate your thoughts (even if you still feel confused) can lead to unexpected connections and even surprising breakthroughs.

Still Stumped? Browse. If you still haven't settled on a topic that seems interesting enough, try browsing an encyclopedia. The information given will probably prove too general to include in your final project, but the entries can help you discover or personalize a research assignment. You will do more extensive research once you determine your topic, but sometimes an encyclopedia article on a general topic can spark an idea or help you make connections that would not have occurred to you otherwise.

---

e- TIPS

Online Encyclopedias

Britannica.com and ***MSN Encarta,*** once the most commonly used free online encyclopedias, now require subscriptions. However, ***Britannica.com*** <http://www.britannica.com/> includes a search engine that reviews and rates Web sites pertinent to the search topic (see *The Web's Best Sites* box on the search results page). ***Encyclopedia.com*** <http://www.encyclopedia.com/> is still free, and its *e-library* (located at the bottom of the search results page) offers access to current newspaper and magazine articles that provide recent perspectives on a search topic.

For instance, the results of a search using the terms "Vietnam War" and "film" in *The Web's Best Sites* includes a bibliography of a dozen books that discuss how depictions of the war in popular films have altered over the years **(see Figure 1.1).**

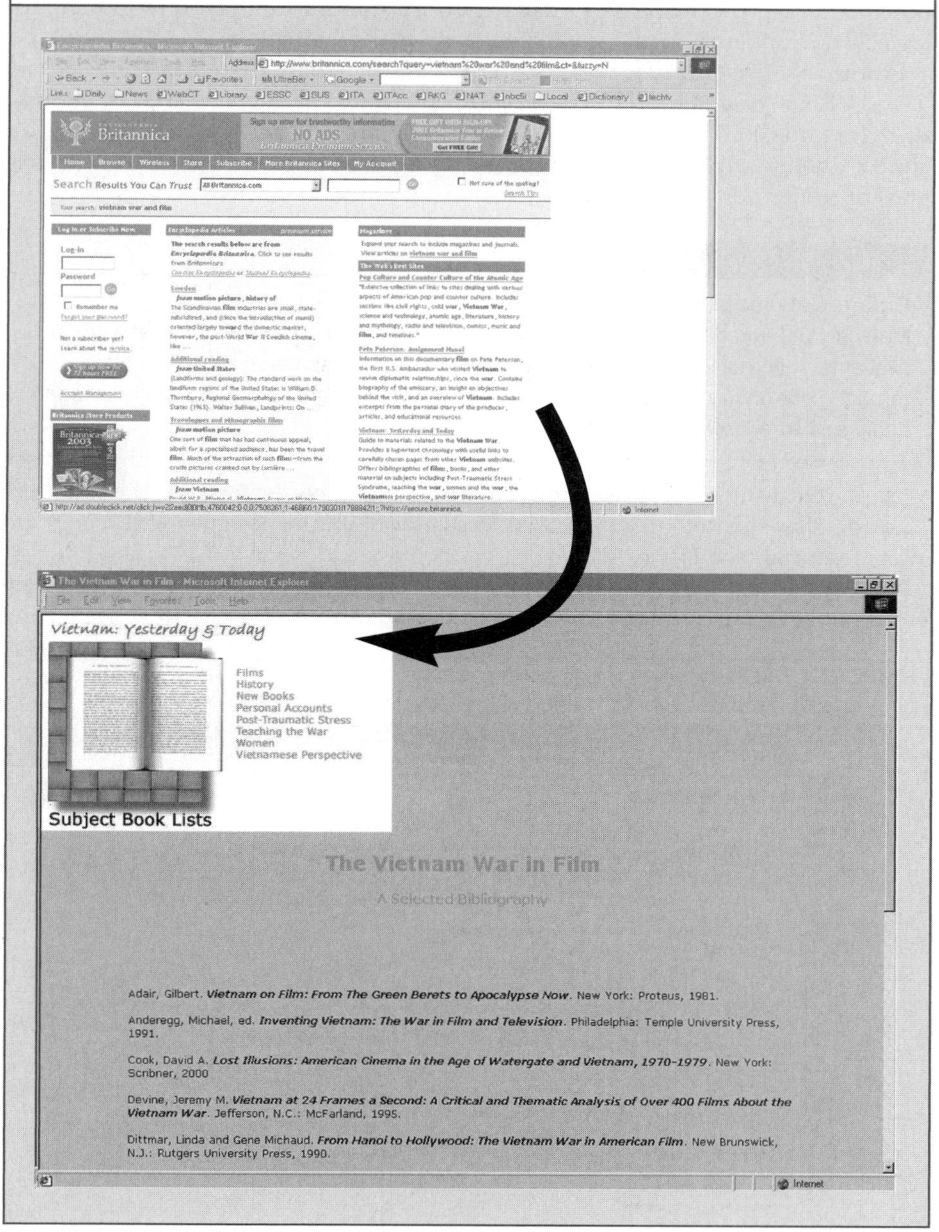

Figure 1.1 The article below, found using an online encyclopedia, provides twelve potential sources for further research.

There is also a short essay on Hollywood's treatment of the war that names particular films and the directors involved. This search using an online encyclopedia combines the assigned topic with a more personal concern to generate a possible research topic (and potential resources for further study). At this stage, you're not really looking for sources (although you might take a few minutes to bookmark or print them out for later use). Most importantly, you're looking for ideas. Time taken to develop your ideas will not be misspent.

Another source for new ideas is a large daily newspaper (such as the *New York Times, Washington Post, Wall Street Journal,* or *Chicago Tribune*). Newspapers, because they are published daily and reflect issues of contemporary concern, provide an almost endless supply of hot topics (i.e., subjects that are currently of interest and/or under debate).

---

e-TIPS

Online Newspapers

Many school libraries now have the *New York Times* and/or the *Wall Street Journal* available online or on a CD-Rom. You might be able to access full-text articles through your online reference system, or your library might have a computer station dedicated to a *Times* or *Journal* database.

A search using the terms "Vietnam War" and "architecture" on the *New York Times* database turned up an interview with Maya Lin, the designer of the Vietnam War Memorial **(see Figure 1.2).**

The article reveals that when the memorial was first proposed, many Vietnam veterans initially were outraged by the design. An analysis of their concerns, the com-

Figure 1.2 This database provides only the bibliographic information. Some libraries have on-site databases that provide full-text articles from the *New York Times.*

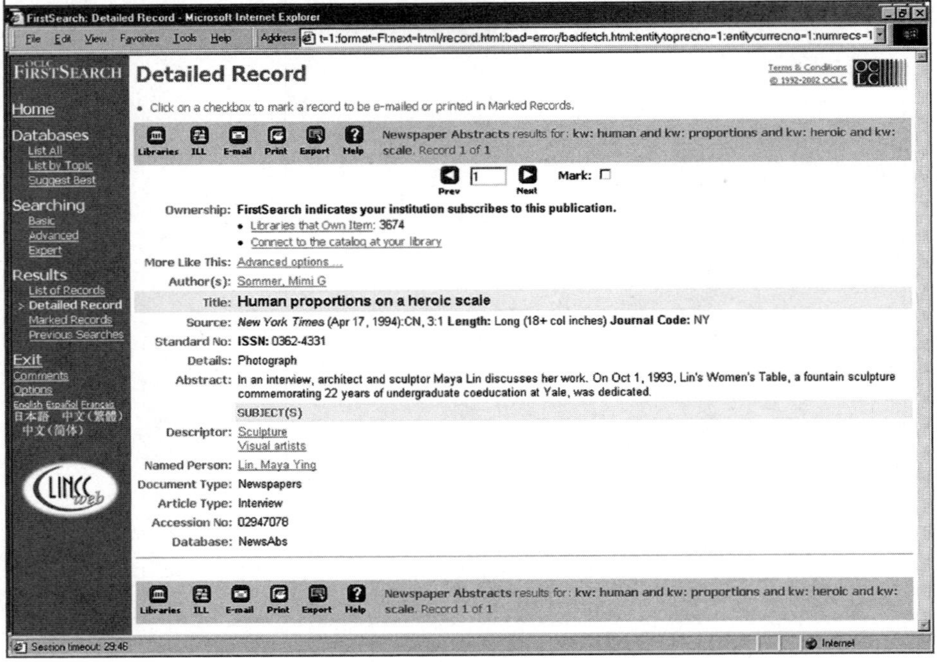

promises that were made, and the present popularity of the memorial (it is one of the most visited sites in the nation's capitol) would be one way of relating the two subjects.

Although an article like this might generate an idea for a topic, you should remember that like encyclopedia entries, newspaper articles might not be the best sources of information for the final research project. Journalists are not usually experts on a topic (although they rely on experts). You would eventually need to learn what experts (i.e., scholars or scientists) are saying through further research. However, this article does supply the seed ideas for a research project that merges an assigned subject (the Vietnam War) with an individual interest (architecture).

The Internet is not usually the best starting point for extensive research on a topic because it is frequently difficult to determine whether information on a Web site is reliable. But if you have tried everything else and are still casting about for an idea, the Web (like an encyclopedia or popular periodical) can help you determine a direction for your project. A simple keyword search will sometimes reveal interesting viewpoints and ideas.

For example, a quick search using the key terms "Vietnam War" and "medicine" turned up an informative Web site on the effects of Agent Orange **(see Figure 1.3)**. Compiled by four veterans who are interested in getting information to others who might have been affected by Agent Orange, this site documents that although America's involvement in the war ended in 1975, the United States government did not take definitive action to aid ailing veterans until the release of

Figure 1.3 This Web site is exhaustively documented, offering government reports as well as analysis and opinion.

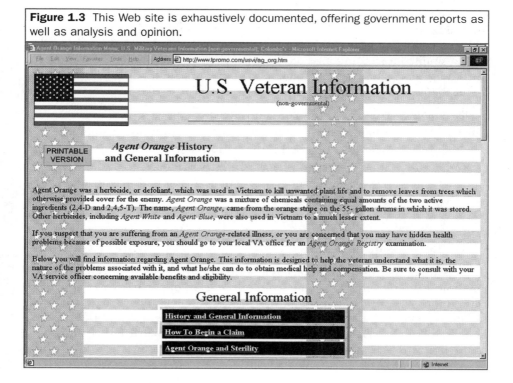

a study in 1993. This study linked Agent Orange to a host of serious health problems. One research question that arises immediately would be "Why the delay?" An investigation of the reasons for this time lapse might intrigue a premed or a prelaw student.

If you choose to use the Internet at this stage, remember that you are just *browsing* to find a topic. You will need to focus your topic more fully before you can begin to research in earnest.

ℓ- TIPS

Search Engines

All search engines are not created equal. Some search word-for-word through the entire text, others organize Web sites into categories, and some are directories that do not search the entire Web. When *browsing,* your best choice would be a subject directory such as ***Librarians' Index*** <http://www.lii.org>, ***Infomine*** <http://infomine.ucr.edu/>, ***Yahoo*** <http://www.yahoo.com>, or ***Galaxy,*** <http://galaxy.com/> or a subject guide like ***About.com*** <http://www.about.com.>

Choose a Worthwhile Topic

In addition to being relevant to you personally, an academic research project must fulfill the expectations of your instructor. The best topics invite discussion or debate and don't just recycle popular opinion (which may or may not be knowledgeable or informed) or regurgitate facts. You should choose a topic that will involve you in an interesting quest for knowledge and understanding rather than a simple fact-finding mission. Your research project should be stimulating for the reader as well as the writer, and the best ones almost always ask questions about the *how* or *why* of something—not just *what* or *where.*

Too Simple:	What TV shows contain violence?
	What e-commerce businesses have proven successful?
	Where are the best hospitals located?
Worthwhile:	Should television networks restrict violent programming in response to objections by religious and parental advocacy groups?
	Why have certain e-commerce businesses been successful?
	How have the best hospitals in the country achieved their superior status?

So think of the research project as an opportunity to find out something new about an issue that intrigues you. Think of it as an opportunity to help you to think more complexly about important issues, events, and ideas. It might be tempting to choose a topic quickly so you can get to the "real" work of finding books and articles and writing your report. However, if you rush this initial stage of the project, you might soon become discouraged and bored.

Step 2: Narrow Your Focus

Even if you choose a focus for your paper that is personally interesting, if you do not adequately narrow the subject of your research, you will sabotage your project. Students often make the mistake of keeping their topics very broad and general, reasoning that they will run out of things to say if they choose a more focused or narrow subject. The best research papers begin with a carefully delineated assertion that is then methodically substantiated by specific examples and evidence. If you begin with a broad assertion, you will be hard pressed to provide adequate (or interesting) support for all that you claim. When it comes to research papers, it is generally better to say *a lot about a little* rather than *a little about a lot*.

Too Broad: Children should have rights in our society.

Focused: School locker searches are unconstitutional.

   or   Drug testing should be banned from high school sports.

   or   Teen curfews are undemocratic.

   or   High school newspapers should not be censored by the administration.

⏱ *Quick* CHECK

Determine Project Scope
The BEST topics are specific and focused.
- Restrict your project to a topic/task you can complete successfully.
- Determine the scope of your topic to meet
  - the assigned length of the project
  - the time you have to complete the project
  - the resources you have at your disposal

Remember three important factors when determining the scope of your project.

1. *The assigned length of the project:* From the beginning, choose a topic that suits the limits of your assignment. If your instructor expects a ten-page essay, then your topic needs to be sufficiently complex. On the other hand, choose a less involved subject if the assignment is only three to five pages long; otherwise you will only scratch the surface of your topic. For example, in ten to fifteen pages you could create a credible argument supporting the need for laws that require children to wear helmets when bicycling. If the assigned length is three pages, you might choose to narrow your subject to a discussion of how helmets have proven to protect children involved in bicycling accidents.

2. *The time you have to complete the project:* Any research project is time consuming. Certain topics will require even greater amounts of time. If your topic requires interviewing experts or conducting surveys and compiling results, you need to allow time for this. Regardless of the type of research you are doing, make sure you limit your topic so you will have enough time to gather the necessary information. For instance, you might be interested in investigating the effectiveness of stalking laws. One way to make this subject more manageable would be to limit your discussion to the success rate of such laws in your own state or municipality.

3. *The resources you have at your disposal:* The Internet has made it possible to obtain a great deal of information that was formerly inaccessible or available only through interlibrary loan. Nevertheless, if you choose a topic that is so current or unstudied that little information about it exists, you will not be able to find enough information to support a research paper.

A few years ago, MP3s (digital recordings available via the Internet) were just beginning to surface, and little information (beyond explanations of what they are and how they operate) existed. A researcher would have been frustrated by the quantity and quality of the information available. However, because of the threat MP3s pose to the multimillion-dollar recording industry, recently there has been a great deal of discussion about the commercial impact and ethical concerns surrounding this phenomenon. Today, a student who chose this topic would find numerous sources with far-ranging opinions **(see Figure 1.4).**

Conscientious research requires that you become acquainted with a variety of perspectives on your subject. Therefore, if after extensive investigation you discover there is insufficient dialogue on the topic, you must reject it or refocus

Figure 1.4 A search in this database revealed 489 periodical articles on MP3s. Prior to 1999 (when MP3s were first marketed), there was very little written about these recordings.

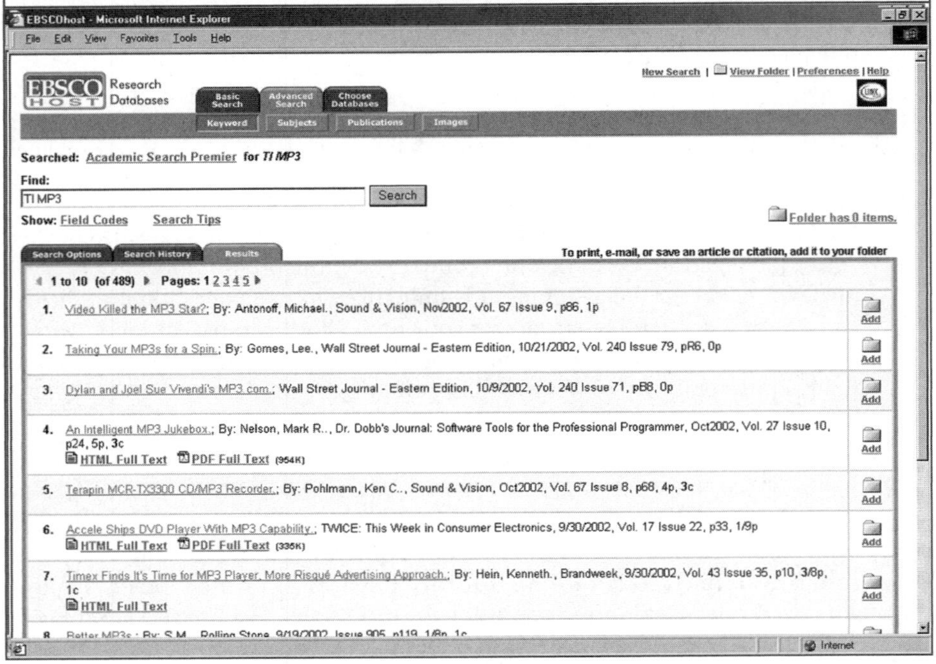

it in a more promising direction. Once you have chosen a topic and narrowed your focus, you are ready to begin to explore the different types of sources available (e.g., books, periodicals, Web sites, interviews, surveys). As your familiarity with various resources develops, you may develop an individualized approach to this process. However, certain time-tested strategies will remain constant. These research strategies are discussed in the following chapters.

Exercises

1. People write best when they choose topics that fascinate them; however, in order to choose a relevant topic, you need to know yourself. To help you understand your interests, complete the following phrases as honestly and completely as you can.

   - The subject I most enjoy reading about is . . .
   - My favorite hobby or pastime is . . .
   - If I won the lottery, I would use the money to . . .
   - The type of volunteer activity I prefer is . . .
   - My favorite school subject has always been . . .
   - If I ran the world, the first thing I would change would be . . .

2. Your biology professor has assigned a research paper on "biological warfare." To get an overview of this topic and to begin to determine the specific focus for your project, access an online encyclopedia (<www.britannica.com>; <www.encyclopedia.com>) and enter the search phrase "biological warfare." Make full use of the features provided by these tools (see "e-tip" on page 6; consult *The Web's Best Sites* in **Britannica.com;** check the *e-library* in **Encyclopedia.com**) to locate as much current information as possible. As you browse these resources, keep in mind the interests you identified in Exercise 1 and list two potential topics or research questions that combine your personal interests with the issue of biological warfare.

3. The *InfoTrac*® database can also help you determine a particular focus for a project. Use the passcode provided with this text to access the database and conduct a search using the same phrase ("biological warfare") as the previous exercise. [Use the "Easy Search" function and conduct a "Subject Guide" search.] Browse down the results page and click on the listing entitled "Subdivisions." Review this inventory of categories and select three that interest you for further study. List these, and briefly (in a sentence or two) explain why they attracted your attention.

4. Return to the same "results" list from your search on "biological warfare" in Exercise 3 and click on "Related Subjects" (this appears just below the "Subdivisions" link). Choose ONE of these related subjects (the one that seems most intriguing to you) and then click on the "Subdivisions" link for this topic. Write a paragraph that explains why you chose this particular "Related Subject" (stipulate what made it more interesting to you than the others). Also indicate which ONE of the subdivisions under this subject seems most interesting to you and why.

CHAPTER TWO

Find the Perfect Match

"What is research, but a blind date with knowledge?"

WILLIAM HENRY

Don't let the chapter title fool you—we're still talking about research projects, not dating. But once you choose a topic for your research project, you must then find the information you need to answer your research questions. This means you will need to determine which key terms and phrases are most likely to guide you to that information. Sometimes that can be almost as difficult as finding Mr. or Ms. Right.

Where Do You Find the Perfect Match?

The Internet: Great Source or Source of Great Confusion?

In many ways, the Internet has made it easier to conduct research. The "Information Superhighway" can, with the click of a mouse, help you connect and communicate with countless potential sources for your investigation. Before the development of this system, students were usually limited to the resources available in their school and public libraries or through interlibrary loan. (Back then, even if the information was available, it usually took longer to find.) Today, you also have the options of accessing resources from the libraries of other colleges or universities **(see Figure 2.1),** e-mailing (or even conducting an online discussion with) a noted expert on your topic, joining a list serve comprised of others interested in your subject, as well as browsing a billion Web pages. However, while the Internet has greatly expanded your choices for conducting research, it has also created new problems for the novice researcher.

Three Common Problems with Internet Searches

Too Many Web Sites, Too Little Time. The most common complaint students have is the sheer number of "hits" they get when conducting a keyword search. A search for a specific subject or item can turn up hundreds, or even thousands, of Web sites, and sifting through all of these options is a time-consuming task. Although search engines are great for obtaining certain types of information

Figure 2.1 This Web site offers links to almost 100 online catalogues including United States colleges and universities, public libraries, and international libraries.

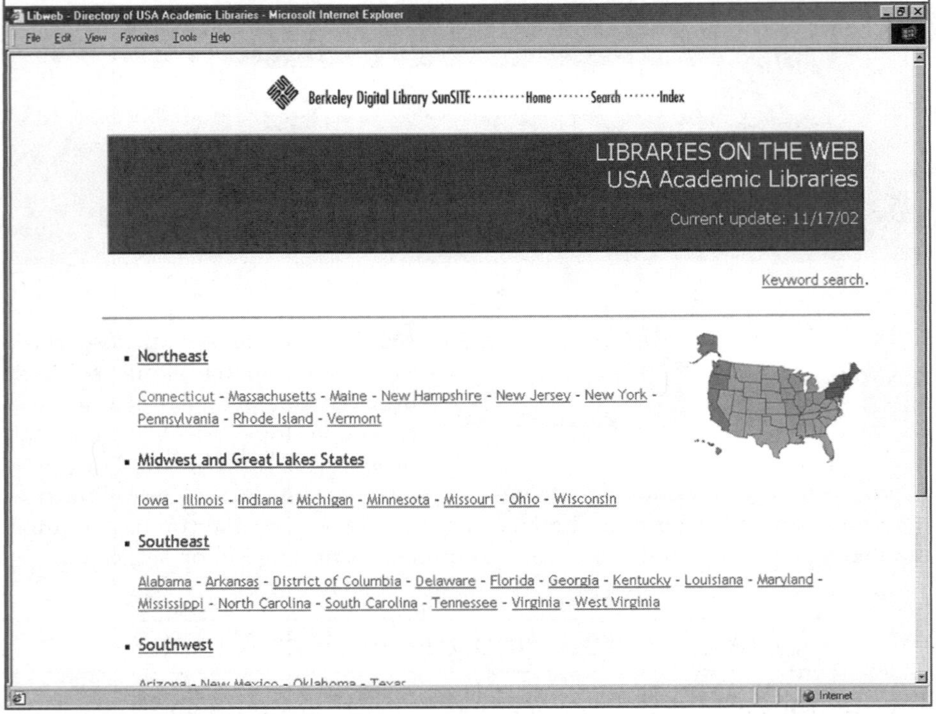

(e.g., which camera is best suited to your photography needs), much of the research you will be required to do during your academic career might be too complex and nuanced for a simple search using *Yahoo, MSN.Search, Google,* or any of the other commercial search engines commonly employed to surf the Web.

Unsuitable Web Sites. Another related problem is that your search will probably return numerous sites that are unrelated to your topic. This is because search engines are operated by "robots" (sometimes called "spiders" or "worms")— computer programs that roam the Web, locating and cataloging sites with little or no human intervention. These robots rely on word choice and frequency of word use to determine what constitutes a match, but have little sense of context. In addition, because many Web editors want to increase the number of visitors to their sites for advertising purposes, they often embed invisible word lists that deceive these robots into making false matches. As a result, you can waste a great deal of time looking at irrelevant sites **(see Figure 2.2).**

Unreliable Web Sites. Although the previous problems may make your Internet searches frustrating and time consuming, perhaps nothing undermines an aca-

Figure 2.2 A simple Internet search using the keywords "bicycle helmets" resulted in 472,000 matches.

demic research project more absolutely than the failure to identify inappropriate sources published on the Web. The Internet has made it possible for anyone with rudimentary computer skills and a URL to publish information to a vast audience. In the past, most students collected the bulk of their information from school or public libraries. They could assume that these resources were reliable because editors of publishing companies, peer experts, and librarians had already evaluated them. However, no such methods of control determine what's published on many, if not most, Web sites. A student researcher must personally evaluate each Web page to determine if the information is accurate and reliable. This is not always easy to discern, and it makes any research done on the Web particularly challenging.

The Solution: Begin Your Research in the Library

For these reasons, although you may eventually discover helpful resources on the Internet, the library remains the best *starting point* for conducting academic research. Internet technologies have transformed our libraries, making it possible to conduct searches more quickly and to access materials more easily. However, unlike the World Wide Web, your library's online reference system and bank of databases will most likely be current, credible, and relevant because they are largely devoted to scholarly and/or reputable sources. **For almost all research projects you will encounter during your college career, the best place to** *begin* **your search will be your school library's online reference catalog.**

---

e- TIPS

Using an Online Library Catalog

Some online reference catalogs can be accessed only from computer terminals located in the school's library, but many colleges and universities have connected their catalogs to the Web, making it possible for students to conduct research from non-networked computers. You still have to visit the library to check out books and access many of the holdings, but for numerous activities you are no longer restricted to the hours your library is open.

Also, college and university libraries often charge fees for printing research materials from school computers. Printing bibliographies of potential resources or full-text articles can be expensive. However, many online systems allow you to e-mail your search findings (which you can then print at your home computer). You may want to do the bulk of your searching from a computer with free or relatively inexpensive printing.

Types of Library Resources. Computers have changed the way we use our libraries; they have made it easier to use many library resources whenever, or from wherever, we choose. Nonetheless, in many ways library holdings have remained constant. There are still three main types of resources: general and special reference works, books, and periodicals. What can be confusing is differentiating between your school's physical library (the actual building where books and periodicals are housed) and the virtual library, which usually includes the online catalog and databases (online resources your library has purchased and made available on-site or through links to its Web site) and which can include many additional study helps. Internet technology has made it possible for even small libraries to offer impressive collections.

You will need to visit your library in person to check out books and periodicals, but with today's technology, library resources (and your access to them) have been greatly expanded. You might already have a preference for the types of materials you like to use (probably because you have experienced success with one type when doing a research project in the past), but don't limit yourself. One way to gain a less biased perspective in your research is to gather information from a variety of sources. Learn to use all of the resources available to you.

- General and Special Reference Works. Every library has a reference section. It is usually located in an especially accessible area, often near the front of the library. Books in this section (which include encyclopedias, dictionaries, atlases, almanacs, and biographical references) cannot be checked out. You may not realize it, but reference sections also include special reference works. These are encyclopedias, dictionaries, and other similar tools devoted to specific disciplines. At some point early in your college career, browse the reference section to get a sense of the resources available, especially those specific to your major. Some of these reference works (like general encyclopedias and dictionaries) are now available online, (see the E-Tips on pages 6 and 8 about online newspapers and encyclopedias) but many special reference works are still accessible only by visiting your library. Here is a sampling of the types of special reference works that might be housed in the General Reference section.

- *Business and the Environment: a Resource Guide*
- *The Bulfinch Guide to Art History: a Comprehensive Survey and Dictionary of Western Art and Architecture*
- *From Suffrage to the Senate: an Encyclopedia of American Women in Politics*
- *Dictionary of Mathematics*

Because its resources will provide general overviews of your topic, the reference section can be an excellent starting point for your research; however, you will want to expand your search for information beyond these sorts of general resources.

- Books. You are probably most familiar with these holdings. In fact, when you hear the word "library," books are what probably leap to mind. Library books are housed in the "stacks" (the main bookcases of the library), are arranged according to subject categories determined by the Library of Congress, and can be checked out and removed from the library.

---

e- TIPS

Interlibrary Loan

The Internet has made interlibrary loans much easier. Some schools even allow you to order interlibrary loans online. Also, check to see if your school has agreements with other colleges or universities to share library resources. In my state, the colleges have linked their online catalogs so students can search just their own or all of the libraries for materials. It also has an arrangement with a neighboring university so that students can check out books from its much larger collection. Interlibrary loans from these schools often take less than a week to complete.

- Periodicals. Periodicals are publications such as newspapers, magazines, and scholarly journals that are issued at regular intervals (e.g., daily, weekly, monthly). You might be familiar with periodicals like the *New York Times, Newsweek,* and *U.S. News and World Report;* however, you may be less familiar with the many scholarly periodicals available in your library. The articles in these journals are written by experts in their fields, rather than reporters, and often provide the most up-to-date information on a subject because they are published more quickly than books. Periodicals, because they are frequently published on more perishable materials, are also the most "polymorphous" holdings in the library—you may find them available in their original "hard" (or printed on paper) state, on microfiche, on microfilm, or increasingly, in computer databases.

Full-Text Databases

Many smaller libraries have limited periodical resources. However, a new breed of databases (e.g., *WilsonSelect, SIRSResearcher, Academic Search Elite [EBSCOhost]*, *InfoTrac® [Gale], Business Source Premier (EBSCOhost), Career and Technical Education [ProQuest]*, etc.) offers full-text periodical articles. How to use these databases will be discussed more fully in future chapters.

How Do You Find the Perfect Match?

Become Familiar with Your Library's Online Reference Catalog

Library research used to mean hours spent shuffling through stacks of index cards in drawer after drawer of the card catalog. However, computers have made the card catalog a thing of the past, and almost *all* library reference systems are now electronic. Learning to use your school's online catalog has a number of benefits that go beyond the obvious one of locating books, journal articles, or other resources available through your library system. It offers the perfect starting point for learning to effectively use electronic search tools **(see Figure 2.3)**.

Understand Electronic Search Tools

Although computer search tools may differ slightly in appearance and the features they offer, they all operate similarly. Whether you are using an Internet search engine, a database, or an online reference catalog, you simply type in a keyword or phrase that identifies the subject in which you are interested, click on a "begin search" button, and then wait for the computer to list all of the documents that match your request.

When you are using an online reference catalog search tool, you can search according to a key term (or subject), an author's name, or the title of the work. Some search tools offer other options as well, but these are the main categories for which you will usually search. At the beginning of a research project you will primarily use the **keyword** or **subject** option. However, although the operation seems very simple, if you have used such a search tool, you know that success or failure depends on your ability to match your search terms with the documents you are trying to retrieve. Even simple spelling errors can block your efforts. A student in one of my classes once spent a very frustrating 40 minutes in the online reference catalog and then brusquely informed me that our library contained absolutely nothing about Albert Einstein. I was a bit mystified until I looked at his computer screen and saw that he had been using the search terms *Albert Einstine*. When he corrected his error he, of course, had a host of documents to choose from. But even if you spell correctly, the most effective search terms may not be the ones that immediately come to mind.

Figure 2.3 Online reference catalogs allow you to search by subject keyword, author, or title. The search screen for your library's catalog might appear slightly different from this, but most operate very similarly.

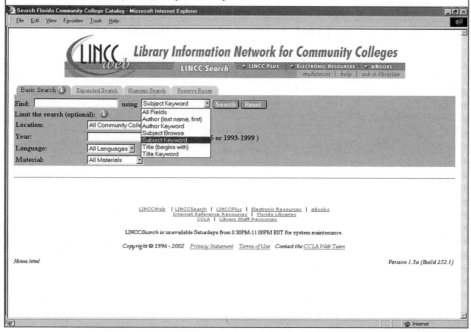

Common Search Mistake

Electronic search tools seek pr＿ ＾ matches to your search terms or phrases. Besides spelling mistakes, anothei ＾mon error students sometimes make is to capitalize words that are not proper n＿ Remember that some search engines are *case sensitive;* only capitalize when a＿ ＾riate.

Formulate Effective Search Terms

The problem with electronic search tools is that althoug＿ ＾ey are much quicker and usually more thorough than humans, they can't thi＿ That is your job. However, this is not to say that you are confined to your own ＾rhaps limited) understanding of your topic. There are numerous support syste＿ ＾vailable to help you assemble a list of possible search words and phrases. **Remen.＿ to keep a running list of possible search terms and phrases as you try, by trial a＿ error, to find keywords that match your topic.** A keyword that was unsuccessful in the online catalog might work in a database or Internet search engine. It takes very little time to jot down a word or phrase, and it could save you much time and effort later. There are a number of ways you can expand your list of keywords.

⏻ Quick CHECK

Identifying Keywords

Identify keywords that match your topic.
- Locate synonyms and alternative phrases for your topic.
- Discover the Library of Congress subject headings that address your topic.
- Combine your search terms into effective Boolean search phrases

Keep a running list of all search terms and phrases because different keywords will be successful in different research tools.

Identify Synonyms or Related Words or Ideas. You might have chosen a topic for which you can readily identify keywords. For example, if you chose to research reasons why marijuana should be legalized for medical purposes, the key terms *marijuana, legalization,* and *medicine* almost leap out at you. Even in this fairly straightforward example, however, there are certain pitfalls you need to be familiar with. For instance, marijuana can also be spelled *marihuana.*

However, not all topics translate so quickly into search terms that will result in finding the information you need. If, for instance, you chose to investigate how communities regulate dog and cat populations, you might try the term *animal control.* Although this might seem like the obvious term (after all, agencies responsible for catching stray dogs and cats are often called *animal control* by local governments), a search using this phrase turned up documents that dealt with livestock, laboratory animals, and wild animals, but nothing about controlling stray or homeless pets.

You have two choices at this point. On the one hand, you could (like my student who informed me that he couldn't locate anything about Albert Einstein) foolishly decide that your library has no information on your topic. The better solution is to discover alternative words or phrases that relate to your subject. For instance, stray cats and dogs are frequently held in *animal shelters,* and in some areas of the country these shelters are run by *humane societies.*

Sometimes a dictionary or thesaurus can help you locate a successful keyword. One of my students wanted to examine how United States colleges and universities are responding to the special problems of foreign students who choose to

---

𝓮- TIPS

Use a Thesaurus

Most word-processing programs include a thesaurus. These computer versions often have shorter lists of optional words than their hard-copy counterparts, but they are much easier to use. Also, scanning alternative words for the synonyms in the original list can lead you to additional lists of possible keywords.

study here. Searches using the phrase *foreign students* resulted in no matches. After consulting a thesaurus for synonyms, she experienced success with the phrase *international students*.

Refer to the Library of Congress Classification System. Because all materials in the library are organized according to standardized categories (unlike the Internet, which is a wild and unregulated virtual space in which documents might be organized under any number of terms or phrases), the Library of Congress classification system can help you discover the key terms and phrases used by academics to describe your topic and match you up with the best resources available. You will find the *Library of Congress Subject Headings* (a four-volume work) in the reference section of your library. It can help you discover optional terms for your topic that you might not have thought of on your own.

---

e-TIPS

Library of Congress Classifications
Your reference librarian can direct you toward a list of Library of Congress subject categories, but you can also find these online. See *LC Classification Outline* at
<http://www.tlcdelivers.com/tlc/crs/lcso0001.htm> or *About.com*'s list at
<http://geography.about.com/library/congress/bllc.htm>

Suppose you are investigating the way fashion reflects contemporary culture's preoccupation with technology. Looking up "fashion" in the *Library of Congress (LC) Subject Headings* would lead you to the terms "Manners and Customs" (the general heading) and "Costume," "Dress," "Materials and articles of clothing," and "Ornaments," alternatives that might be more successful because they are more narrowly focused on your topic. Part of investigating a new subject is learning the language used by those who are experts in that field. Use the well-established subject categories of your library to help you identify the words that will call up the best information when you search (**see Figure 2.4** on page 24).

Construct Boolean Search Phrases. I still remember the first time I heard about a *Boolean search*. The name alone was intimidating. When the librarian (by way of explanation) distributed four or five handouts filled with confusing Venn diagrams, I thought that I would never be able to understand, much less construct, one. I've always been a bit math impaired, and this sounded and looked like something from a statistics or calculus class. Imagine my surprise when I discovered that the idea is very simple. In fact, if you do much surfing on the Web, you have probably already done a Boolean search.

I became less frightened when I realized that the system's odd-sounding name was merely the result of having been created by George Boole. Even though Boole was a mathematician (thus the Venn diagrams), you don't have to be a rocket scientist to understand the process. A Boolean search refines your quest by linking keywords with **AND, OR,** or **NOT** to demonstrate the relationships between the

Figure 2.4 The subject categories listed in the *LC Classification Outline* suggest narrowly focused terms under more general topics.

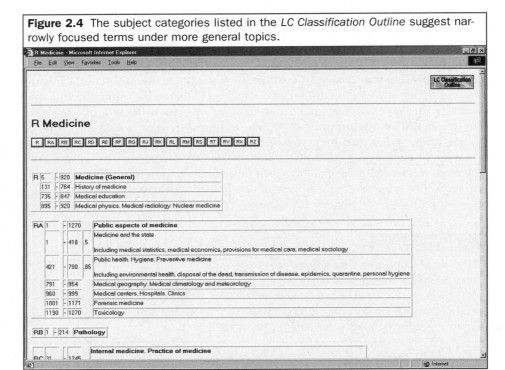

terms. Most research projects have a narrow focus, and Boolean phrases allow you to pinpoint documents that directly address your topic.

A few years ago a student who worked in a pet store decided to investigate the federal law that forbids the sale of turtles under four inches in size. The law was enacted to protect consumers from the threat of salmonella poisoning. Her argument was that the law, although well meaning, was illogical. Salmonella can be spread by any number of reptiles (not just turtles), and

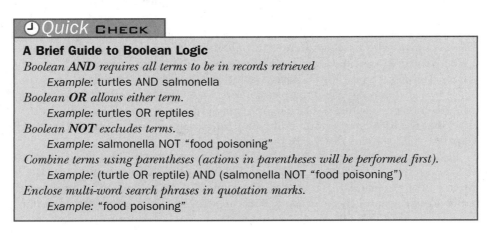

① *Quick* CHECK

A Brief Guide to Boolean Logic

*Boolean **AND** requires all terms to be in records retrieved*
    Example: turtles AND salmonella
*Boolean **OR** allows either term.*
    Example: turtles OR reptiles
*Boolean **NOT** excludes terms.*
    Example: salmonella NOT "food poisoning"
Combine terms using parentheses (actions in parentheses will be performed first).
    Example: (turtle OR reptile) AND (salmonella NOT "food poisoning")
Enclose multi-word search phrases in quotation marks.
    Example: "food poisoning"

infection is not limited to small turtles. After compiling a simple list of keywords *(turtles, reptiles, salmonella),* she organized them into search phrases using the Boolean term **AND** (Boolean terms are always capitalized to distinguish them from the keywords), indicating that both terms in the following examples should appear in the document.

- turtles **AND** salmonella
- reptiles **AND** salmonella

However, when my student attempted to use these Boolean phrases in her school's online catalog, there were no matches. Although these terms are clearly connected to the topic (and may prove productive in another search engine), they did not trigger the desired response in the online library catalog. Therefore, this researcher had to rethink her list of keywords. Her first strategy was to abandon the Boolean terms and conduct a simple keyword search using just the term *turtle.* However, this proved unfruitful because there were too many hits (**see Figure 2.5**). The solution to this problem is not to think more generally but to determine how the information you are looking for specifically differs from what you are finding.

A quick look at the results of the *turtle* keyword search reveals documents about sea turtles, fictional turtles, Ninja turtles, and by publishers with the word *turtle* in their name. When I asked this student how these "turtles" differed from

Figure 2.5 A search using the term *turtle* produces 322 hits, and the first four documents seem totally unrelated to the topic.

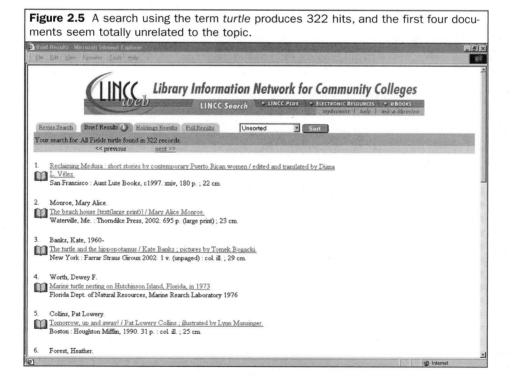

what she was searching for, she readily answered that she was searching for "pet" turtles. She conducted two new Boolean searches:

- turtles **AND** pets
- reptiles **AND** pets

These searches returned documents that were more useful (**see Figure. 2.6**).

Combining phrases is a way to *refine* your search. By this I mean that a Boolean search weeds out unrelated documents and produces matches that directly address your topic. The two preceding searches could be combined into one by using the Boolean term **OR** (use a parenthesis to group search phrases).

- (turtles **OR** reptiles) **AND** pets

My student soon determined that she needed to learn more about salmonella (how it is transmitted, the symptoms, treatment, etc.). She conducted a simple search using the keyword *salmonella* and soon discovered that food poisoning, as well as reptiles, can cause salmonella. Therefore, she refined her search by excluding the terms "food poisoning" (multiword search terms should be enclosed in quotation marks) by using the Boolean term **NOT**:

Figure 2.6 The results of the search for **reptiles AND pets** include only sixteen documents, and the titles indicate that they are specifically related to the researcher's topic.

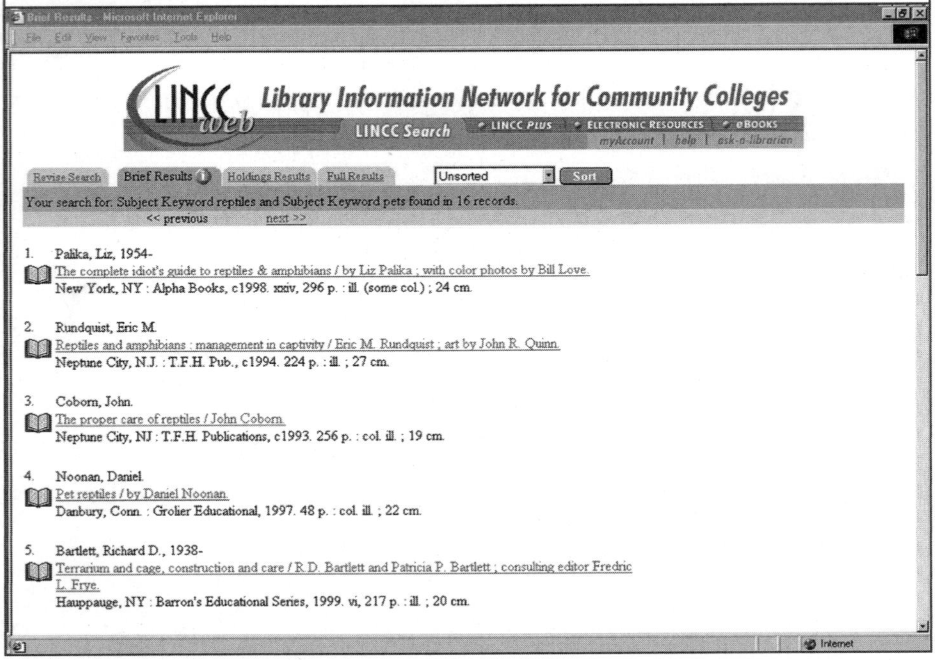

- salmonella **NOT** "food poisoning"

Electronic search tools vary. Some allow you to use complicated search phrases; others can't respond to more than one or two Boolean terms per search. It would be ideal if you could conduct a search such as the following.

- (turtles **OR** reptiles) **AND** (salmonella **NOT** "food poisoning")

Sometimes online search tools allow you to do such advanced searches. It will take a certain amount of trial and error to determine what works best in your library's system.

Boolean searches are simple if you remember four basic rules:

1. Use the Boolean terms **AND, OR,** or **NOT** to specify the relationships between keywords:

- Use AND when you want both keywords to appear in the document: **turtles AND pets.** [Note: Some search tools require a plus sign (+) instead (e.g., turtles + pets).]
- Use OR when either keyword can appear in the document: **turtles OR reptiles.**

Figure 2.7 This online catalog offers a complex search that allows you to refine your query using up to five different Boolean terms.

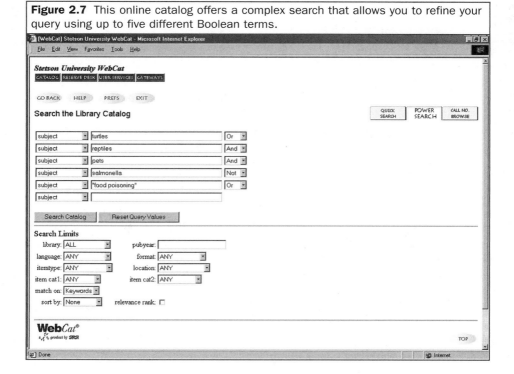

- Use NOT to exclude unwanted terms: **salmonella NOT "food poisoning."** [Note: Some search tools require a minus sign (–) instead (e.g., salmonella – "food poisoning").]

2. Always capitalize Boolean search terms **(AND, OR, NOT)**.

3. Enclose groups of search terms in parenthesis to indicate which actions should occur first: **(turtles OR reptiles) AND salmonella.**

4. Enclose multiword search terms in quotation marks: **salmonella NOT "food poisoning."**

It may not be as exciting as finding that perfect someone, but you will probably feel a certain satisfaction when your keyword and Boolean searches begin to turn up sources that provide the information you need to write a well-documented research essay. As gratifying as this can be, it is only the starting point. The next chapter will discuss how to use your library's resources to continue to expand your search terms and refine your searches, connect with an even greater variety of sources, and evaluate which resources are best for your project.

Exercises

1. The following topics frequently are the subject of student papers. For each of them, write as many synonyms or alternative phrases as you can discover.
   - Mercy killing
   - Teen pregnancy
   - Gun control
   - Antismoking laws
   - War on drugs

2. Using either the *Library of Congress Subject Headings* in your school library's reference section or an online guide (such as <http://lcweb.loc.gov/catdir/cpso/lcco/lcco.html>), locate all of the Library of Congress (LC) subject headings that are pertinent to ONE of the topics listed in Exercise 1. Enter your school's online catalog and use these subject headings as subject search phrases to locate and list four sources that directly address the topic. Print out the complete bibliographic information for these sources.

3. Use the passcode provided with this textbook to access the *InfoTrac®* database and conduct first a "Subject guide" search and then a "Keyword" search (check the appropriate term immediately under the search phrase window) for the phrase "mercy killing" (remember to enclose a multi-word search term in quotation marks). Write a paragraph in which you describe the differences between the two search results and explain why these differences occur.

4. Combine the LC subject headings you identified in Exercise 2 with the synonyms and alternative phrases you discovered for that topic in Exercise 1 to

create as many variant Boolean search phrases as you can. (Refer to the Quick
Check on page 24 for help.) Use the *InfoTrac®* database and experiment
with these search phrases to locate four sources that directly address the
topic. [Note: Databases do not rely on LC subject headings in topic searches.
Nevertheless, identifying the LC headings can help you refine your search.]
Print out the complete bibliographic information for these sources.

CHAPTER THREE

Become a Research "Supersleuth"

"Research is the act of going up alleys to see if they are blind."

PLUTARCH

As Plutarch so aptly noted, the search for relevant information requires a willingness to explore paths that may ultimately lead nowhere. This is especially likely when keywords result in numerous matches; in such cases it's very easy to feel overwhelmed by the sheer amount of information that seems to be available on a topic. Even more frustrating are the odds that many of these seemingly promising hits will not, on further exploration, prove so promising after all. No one wants to spend hours reading a book or article only to reach the conclusion that it isn't pertinent to his or her particular project. But how do you decide early on which sources deserve a closer look and which ones can be ignored? How do you minimize the blind alleys?

This chapter focuses on strategies that can help you zero in on the best leads. I like to compare what researchers do to how detectives work to solve a crime. When a crime is committed, detectives want to pursue only the most promising suspects. Like you, they want to avoid or at least minimize blind alleys or dead ends. Therefore, the first step in any criminal investigation is to develop the clearest and most accurate ideas about the crime, the suspect, and the motive. Expert detectives tirelessly question witnesses, comb the crime scene for clues, and assess possible motives. Taking the time to gather and evaluate evidence is time well spent; it will save valuable time later on. Once detectives have the most accurate picture possible of the crime, the suspect, and the motive, they can limit their search to the most productive leads. In the same way, if you take time at the beginning of a project to clarify your ideas about a topic, develop a working thesis, and then transform that thesis into a series of research questions, you will be well on your way to determining the most direct route to the information you need. Even before you actually begin your "investigation," you will be able to identify whether the resources you discover are likely to be "hot tips" or merely "dead ends."

In short, it pays to know what you are looking for. Of course, in researching, as in sleuthing, sometimes the process is relatively simple and straightforward.

Other times it can be more complex, and you will need to eliminate "red herrings," or false leads, before you find information that will provide the best answers to the questions at hand. In certain cases, what initially seemed irrelevant can even provide the thread that will unravel the mystery at the heart of the investigation. So you might not want to discard or dismiss anything too soon. At the same time, you'll need to avoid using flimsy or erroneous information—often the result of moving too quickly—to construct a false representation or flawed understanding of the subject. In sleuthing, that kind of error can lead to convicting the wrong person (or no conviction at all); in writing and research, it will result in a project that is fundamentally flawed because it ultimately does not establish what it sets out to prove.

Ask Questions

Most detectives begin their investigations by asking questions that will lead them to the perpetrator of the crime: Was anyone seen at or near the scene of the attack? Who would have benefited from the victim's death? Who knew or had access to where the jewelry was stored? You should do likewise, and compose questions that identify what kind of information you need and where you might locate it. What do you need to know before you can make a convincing claim? Which sources are reliable, accurate, and trustworthy? Using these questions to establish an accurate profile early in your investigation will transform your project from a "find a needle in the haystack" experience to a successful "pursuit and capture" of the information you require.

⏱ *Quick* CHECK

Do *Effective* Research
- Transform your research topic into a series of research questions.
- Use research questions to identify new keywords and search phrases.
- Determine what type of information you need to locate.
- Remember that one good source can lead you to another.

What Are You Looking For?

Because all investigations involve locating information that will provide answers to questions, a good way to begin is by transforming your topic or thesis from a statement or assertion into a series of questions. To help you gain this focus, start by asking yourself, "What do I need to know to prove my point?

For example, suppose (like Scott, one of my former students) you are interested in examining the ways federal financial aid programs favor traditional over nontraditional students. Scott had left a job with a good salary to return to school; however, he was shocked to discover that his previous income made him ineligible for financial aid (even though, as a full-time student, he was no longer employed). His experience led him to suspect that the financial aid system gives preference to students who are entering college directly from high school. But how could he be sure? His first attempts at searching in the online catalog produced an overwhelming number of prospective sources **(see Figure 3.1).**

At this point, Scott realized he needed to determine more exactly what information he needed to support his theory. He composed a list of research questions that included the following.

- What are the criteria for financial aid?
- Why do these criteria exist?
- What is a "traditional" student?
- What is a "nontraditional" student?
- In what ways do the financial needs of traditional and nontraditional students differ?
- What assumptions are made by colleges, universities, and financial aid agencies about nontraditional students' needs?

Although he might have been able to give tentative answers to many of these questions before conducting any research, in order to construct a persuasive argument, Scott knew he needed to locate sources that would give him up-to-date information generated by people who had facts to back up their claims. Identifying the specific facts, statistics, definitions, and ideas he was looking for

Figure 3.1 A search of this online catalog using the keywords "student aid" returned an overwhelming number of potential sources. Sifting through all of these possibilities without a clearer agenda would take hours of research time.

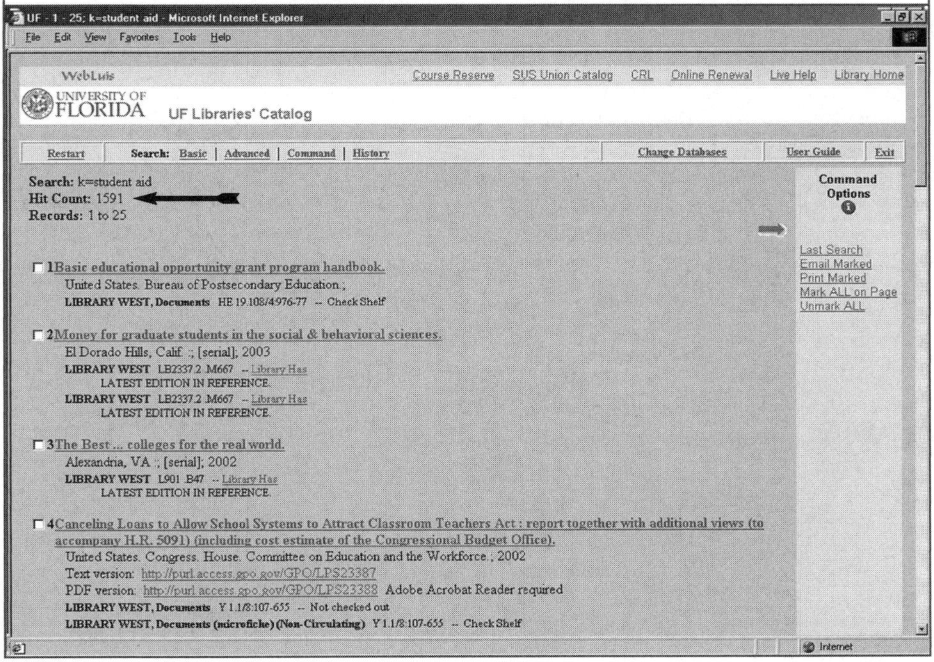

enabled him to sift through the long list of potential sources more selectively. By rephrasing his thesis into a series of questions, his research became *effective* (and by that I mean that he found the best resources available relatively quickly) because he was able to recognize whether the sources he found were trustworthy and whether they provided information relevant to his project **(see Figure 3.2).**

Scott was on the right track. However, he soon discovered that an even more effective method of sleuthing was to use these research questions to identify the keywords and Boolean phrases that would quickly reduce the number of documents the catalog returned. Scott's first search used the keyword phrase *"student aid,"* which produced 1,591 "hits"—too many to sift through! His research questions, however, suggested that he was most interested in a more specific issue, the distribution of financial aid for a particular kind of student. He first tried a Boolean search with the terms *"student aid" AND "nontraditional students,"* but this did not match any of the library subject categories. (If you are unfamiliar with Boolean searches, see Chapter 2.) Undaunted, Scott tried to think of synonyms for the type of student he considered "nontraditional." His subsequent search, using the Boolean phrase *"student aid" AND adults* produced the results he sought **(see Figure 3.3).**

As Scott's experience suggests, carefully composed questions and search terms will help you sift through extraneous information and locate the materials that address your subject directly. Like any good detective, the best researchers and writers are willing to change their minds if confronted with new informa-

Figure 3.2 When the topic is clearly defined, it takes only a quick look at many of these titles to determine whether the sources address the relevant issues.

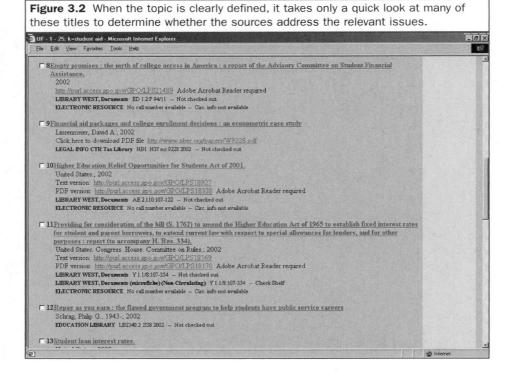

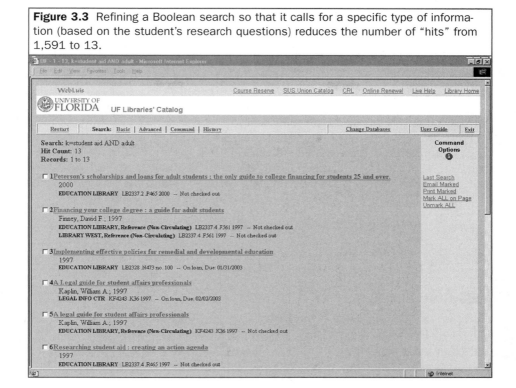

Figure 3.3 Refining a Boolean search so that it calls for a specific type of information (based on the student's research questions) reduces the number of "hits" from 1,591 to 13.

tion. Keep in mind, too, that as you work on the project, your strategies might shift or change as you discover new questions that you need to answer in order to address your subject more fully or successfully. You may even find that the evidence requires modifying your initial thesis. Still, if you don't maintain a clear sense of focus, you will probably feel overwhelmed when you begin to explore online library or Internet resources.

Where Should You Look?

Once investigators determine *who* they are looking for, the next challenge is to ascertain *where* that individual can be found. Police are sometimes able to identify immediately a specific address, but often they have to settle for a more general location such as an area of town or a neighborhood. Likewise, in this early stage of the research process, it is beneficial to think specifically about where you might find the kinds of information you will need to know to make your argument more convincing.

So far, we have only discussed the library online catalog to emphasize basic research strategies. However, there are many other resources to consider, both within the library and in the virtual and real spaces outside it. The next three chapters will discuss how to use databases, the Internet, and personal interviews and surveys to obtain information. You will be a much more effective academic "sleuth" if you take a few minutes before pursuing any of those options to consider very carefully and concretely what type of information you will need to convince a reader that what you are saying about your topic is valid. Is the purpose of your research to locate factual support for a position? To review opinions on a topic? To discover new ideas? To track down eyewitness accounts? To find reasonable arguments on a controversial issue in order to develop your own? If your project requires statistics and facts, the more current they are, the better. In such cases, you might want to use periodicals and/or the Internet to locate the most recent information. Does your project deal with local or regional issues? If it does, you might want to supplement information found in newspapers or government records with interviews or surveys. On the other hand, you may know that your topic has already generated considerable discussion in print. In this case you'll want to use databases and the library catalog to locate relevant texts. Given the nature of college-level writing assignments, most often your research will involve using some combination of these different sources.

Make Connections

Follow the Clues

Experienced detectives know that a successful investigation involves tracking down leads, eliminating red herrings, and following a trail of clues. A dropped matchbook cover leads to a nightclub, which leads to an observant bartender, which leads to a description of a suspect (which, of course, may or may not be accurate). Academic research is similar—one good source will lead you to another. A book might contain an excellent bibliography that yields five or six additional good sources. A periodical article might reference another source that proves even more fruitful than the original.

Like so many other aspects of research, the computer has greatly enhanced our ability to track these sorts of connections. We have already discussed how you can refine your keyword searches to maximize the number of profitable "hits," but what you might not realize is that online catalogs are designed expressly to help you track down promising leads. Because some entries in online catalogs are hyperlinks, a search under one key term will almost always lead to other pertinent sources (and potential keywords).

𝓮-TIPS

Tracking Key Terms

Hyperlinks make it possible to move very quickly through many different keyword and subject category searches. When you find a promising new key term, add it to your list. You might find this search phrase will be successful in a subsequent database or Internet search. Also copy or print out information about any texts that seem appropriate to your search. There is nothing more frustrating than having to go back and spend additional time relocating a source that you spotted in a prior search.

One Good Source Leads to Another

Consider the example of the student who was interested in turtles and salmonella. Her most productive search phrase was *reptiles AND pets,* which returned 13 titles. A quick glance at this list reveals one that seems particularly appropriate—*The Care of Reptiles and Amphibians in Captivity* by Chris Mattison. A click on that title brings up the full-display description that includes a list of subject categories under which this book has been catalogued **(see Figure 3.4).** Two of the subject headings (the ones including the word *amphibian*) broaden the search beyond turtles and reptiles. However, one of them *(Captive reptiles)* appears especially promising. *Captive* expands the search beyond *pets,* but *reptiles* remains focused on the specific type of animals that are the subject of the project.

Clicking on a subject hyperlink takes the researcher to a listing of all of the titles in that category **(see Figure 3.5),** revealing sources that haven't been located in previous searches. Even better, many of these texts seem more narrowly focused on diseases, medical treatments, and health issues of reptiles, indicating that they will likely provide the most useful information.

Depending on how specific your keyword terms are at the beginning of a search, you might repeat this narrowing down process a number of times to locate your best sources.

Figure 3.4 The subject hyperlinks reveal other Library of Congress categories under which this book is catalogued, providing easy access to additional sources that might contain pertinent information.

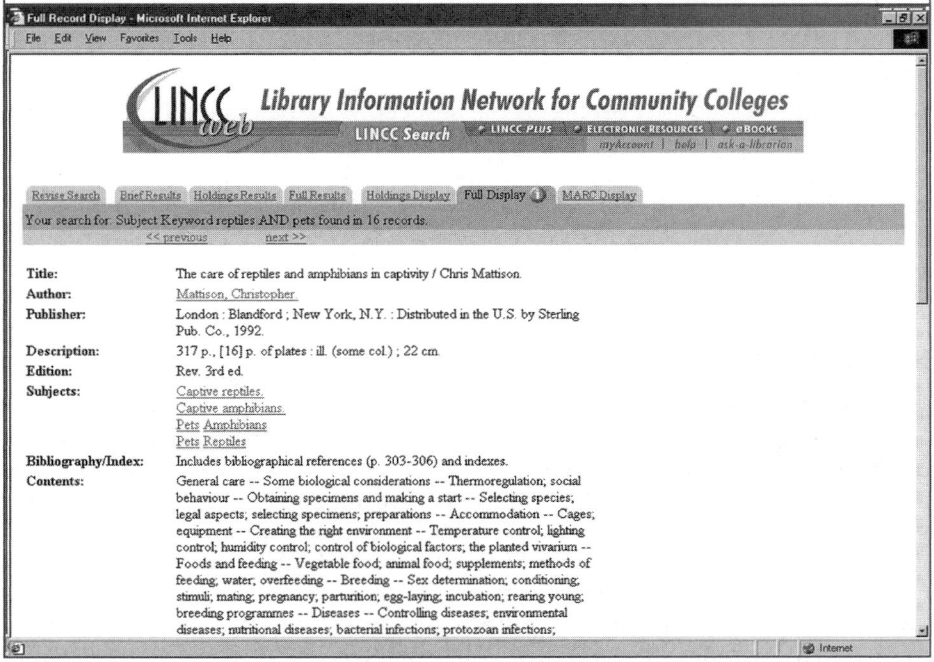

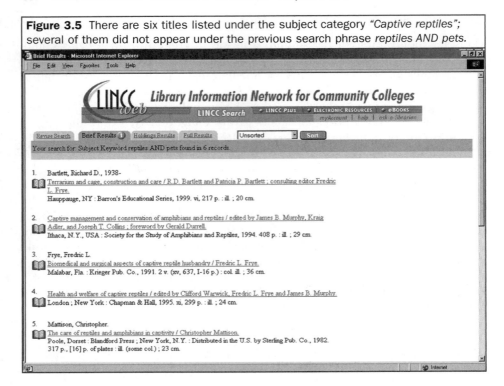

Figure 3.5 There are six titles listed under the subject category *"Captive reptiles"*; several of them did not appear under the previous search phrase *reptiles AND pets*.

Background Checks

In addition to creating a profile of the suspect, working to determine where a suspect might be hiding, and pursuing promising leads, a good detective also runs background checks on people involved with the case. He or she does so to identify individuals with records of criminal activities and/or to determine their credibility. Likewise, academic researchers need to evaluate the "backgrounds" of potential sources to screen out unsuitable or untrustworthy sources and to identify those that are most appropriate and credible.

Evaluation Is an Art

A number of criteria are traditionally used to evaluate sources: purpose, reputation, intended audience, reliability, and timeliness, among others. You will no doubt quickly discover that applying these criteria involves skills that take time and experience to develop. In some ways, learning to evaluate sources is like developing a proficiency in the arts or athletics. A music teacher can instruct you in the basics of playing the clarinet—show you which holes to cover to produce certain notes and how to shape your mouth to accommodate the mouthpiece and reed—but you must practice diligently to learn the subtle control required to make music rather than squawks. A baseball coach can show you the proper stance and how to swing level, but it will take much batting practice before you can step up to the plate with confidence. If you want to hit the ball to a particular spot on the field or play a musical composition with extremely high notes, you will need to learn to make minute adjustments and refine these skills to produce the desired result.

Evaluating sources is much the same. There is no single marker that demonstrates accuracy or appropriateness. Instead, you must analyze a variety of clues in relation to how you plan to use the information. If what you need are facts and statistics, then you will be especially concerned with accuracy, timeliness, and reliability, factors that gauge the quality of your source. If you need an opinion that supports a position, then you want to make sure the source is credible, reasonable, and authoritative. But if you are looking for firsthand experience that is persuasive because it is personal, then it might not matter if the author is renowned. Most research projects use a mix of all these types of sources. A former student who had worked in a day care center wanted to investigate how preschool children were affected by spending 6 to 8 hours away from their parents. The final paper combined facts from recent psychological and sociological studies with the opinions of noted authorities on children and child care, as well as anecdotes from the student's own experience.

As has already been mentioned, you can generally trust information housed in a library because it has undergone a great deal of evaluation. A number of controls ensure the quality of these sources. Textbooks, scholarly studies, and articles in specialized journals have been reviewed by the author's colleagues, editors, and publishers. On the other hand, you should never accept a library source as credible or appropriate just because it is in the library. Keep in mind that information exists in all sorts of forms (stories, reports, arguments, statistics) and is published for a variety of purposes (to express a belief, to entertain, to persuade); therefore, it is important to determine whether a source is suitable for your intended use. *Moby Dick* contains a great deal of information about whales, but you probably wouldn't want to use Melville's novel as a source for a research paper on marine biology.

Internet Sources Require Special Evaluation Skills

Nonetheless, even in the digital age, the library remains an excellent point of departure for the novice researcher because you can have confidence in the reliability of its resources. This is a point worth restating: The library is the best starting place for academic research. Also, library systems have been developed with evaluation in mind. The format of the online catalogue provides you with much of the information you will need to determine the reliability of a text **(see Figure 3.6).**

The World Wide Web is an entirely different matter. Many novice researchers think that Web pages must be reliable because they offer current information and are so easy to access. However, unlike more traditional forms of information media (books, magazines, journals, and government or organization documents), no one regulates information published on the Web, and there is no standard method of cataloguing information. Frequently the indicators needed

Figure 3.6 The listings in an online catalogue provide much of the information you will need to evaluate it (i.e., author, publisher, copyright date, whether it contains references, and a summary of the contents).

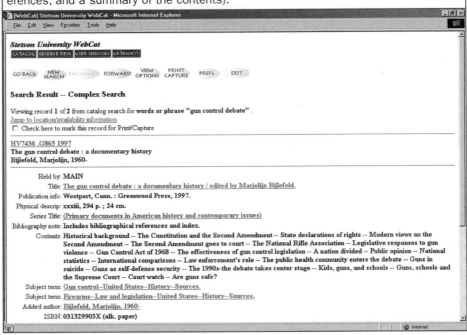

for evaluation (authorship, date of publication, organizational affiliations) are missing. This poses unique problems for research that will be discussed more fully in Chapter 5. But before tackling those more complex situations, it makes sense to learn essential evaluation skills in the user-friendly online catalogue. After all, it's necessary to master the basics before attempting to slam a line drive to the opposite field or hit a C above high G.

Key Factors of Evaluation

When detectives run background checks, they stipulate characteristics (things such as age, sex, race, home address, or even the type of car a person drives) to limit the pool of potential suspects. When it comes to academic research, there are similar indicators that can help you eliminate unlikely sources and locate valuable ones. Your research questions should help you determine whether the basic content matter of a source is relevant, but there are other factors to keep in mind.

When my student was trying to decide whether to use Chris Mattison's text on the care of reptiles for her research project, she had to evaluate whether it was a worthwhile source. The book is part of our school library's holdings—a good sign, but would it be a suitable resource that fulfilled the academic requirements for a scholarly research essay? Like a detective, she needed to be suspicious and not accept this information at face value. So, she asked questions.

⏱ Quick CHECK

Key Factors of Source Evaluation
- What is the purpose of the document?
  - Does it present fact, opinion, or both?
  - Does it maintain a fair, balanced, and reasonable perspective?
- Where does the document come from?
  - Who is the publisher?
  - Who is the author?
- For whom is the document intended?
  - Is it written for a scholarly, college-level audience?
  - Is it too technical or specific for your project?
- When was the document published?
  - Does it include the most up-to-date information available?
  - If dated, does it offer an interesting perspective or point of contrast?
- What does the document look like?
  - Does it look serious and scholarly?
  - Does it have footnotes, a bibliography, an index, and other signs of credibility?
- What do others say about the document?
  - Has it been recommended by an instructor or cited in another, credible source?
  - Is there a review of the source in an abstract or summary?

What Is Its Purpose? This is the first question you should ask when evaluating a potential source. Is it attempting to persuade you to adopt an idea or belief? Is it someone's opinion? Is it a report on facts or findings? Is it an advertisement? All information has a purpose or a goal, and an enormous amount of information in our culture professes to be unbiased but contains a hidden agenda intended to persuade the reader.

If you are trying to decide between buying a Honda Civic or a Mazda Protege, you might visit dealers and obtain brochures. However, unless you are extremely inexperienced, you wouldn't limit yourself to the information a salesperson supplies. The purpose of these brochures is to sell cars; although the facts they contain might be accurate, they are intended to give you the most favorable impression of a vehicle. In fact, most of these publications are carefully contrived to leave you feeling as if your life would be wretched and empty if you did *not* purchase the vehicle. If you want a more accurate picture of how these two cars compare—one that takes limitations as well as advantages into account—you need to refer to *Consumer Reports* or some other less-biased source for information **(see Figure 3.7).**

Even a biased source can be valuable to your research, but only if you recognize its slant. Some writers (published authors as well as students!) are so intent on persuading readers to agree with their opinions that they misrepresent facts or ignore information that challenges their conclusions. Like the car dealer, they want to sell you on an idea without considering other options. To accept what these writers say as unequivocally true will only result in repeating their error.

Figure 3.7 This Web site presents unbiased information that enables consumers to compare the price and features of two similar vehicles.

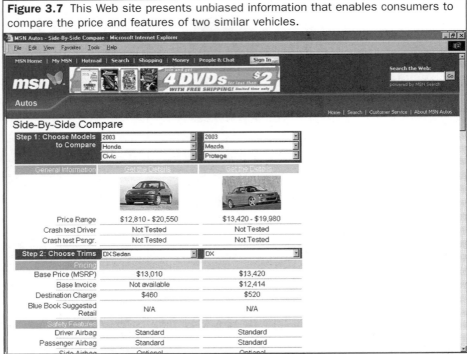

Objectivity and balance are distinguishing features of academic research. A scholarly source will frequently present opinion, but intellectuals are committed to reasoned argumentation that considers (rather than ignores or withholds) conflicting viewpoints. Of course, some topics (such as abortion, capital punishment, and gay marriage) have elicited such extensive, heated, and polarized debate that the only way you will arrive at a balanced understanding is to read widely, becoming familiar with arguments on both sides of the divide.

A sarcastic or superior tone is frequently a sign of bias. Rather than draw on established facts and reasonable argument, writers with strong bias frequently resort to rude put-downs to discredit contradictory views. Television and radio talk shows have made us all too accustomed to this type of discourse. However, if the author of a source sounds like he or she could be a guest on *Jerry Springer, Jenny Jones,* or *Howard Stern,* there is good reason to be skeptical. Scholarly writing relies on reason rather than ridicule to make its points. If you are already familiar with your topic, you might recognize serious omissions or distortions. But what if you are unsure whether the writer has been fair? The only way to allay your uncertainty is to run further background checks.

Where Does It Come From? One key to determining whether a source is taking a balanced, objective approach to the subject is to determine who has published it. One of my students recently wrote a research paper arguing against instituting any additional laws restricting the ownership or use of guns. His bibliography listed numerous publications; however, the National Rifle Association (NRA)

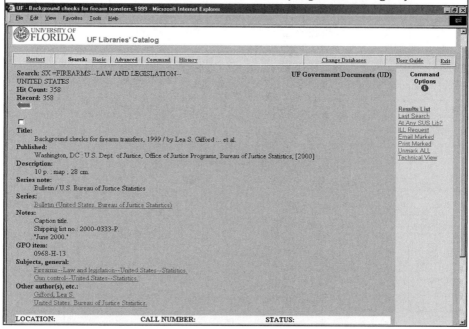

Figure 3.8 The publisher of this bulletin on gun laws is the U.S. Department of Justice. You can be reasonably confident in the accuracy and objectivity of this source because it has been compiled and certified by a government agency.

had published all of them. Because the NRA has invested millions of dollars attempting to block new gun legislation, it can hardly be expected to present all sides of this controversial issue. The information contained in its publications might be technically correct, but the organization's agenda will necessarily shape the argument in explicit and implicit ways. If the publisher is a university press, a well-established publishing company, or a government agency, then you can have greater confidence in the objectivity of the source **(see Figure 3.8).** These organizations carefully examine and review information before affixing their names (and their reputations) to it. If the source is published by an organization, then you need to carefully review its goals and methods of "quality control."

Blandford Press published the book about reptiles that my student was considering using for her research project. This publishing company was unfamiliar to both of us. Therefore, she conducted a quick search on the Internet using the search engine named *Google*.

e- TIPS

Search Engine Tip

Internet search engines are discussed at length in Chapter 5. *Google* is a good choice for this search because "Blandford Press" is a very distinctive search term Notice that this multiword search term is enclosed in quotation marks to indicate that both words should appear as a phrase.

Figure 3.9 The results of an Internet search for "Blandford Press" included references to the Mattison text the student was considering as well as numerous titles unrelated to the topic published by the same company.

She wasn't able to locate a company Web site, but the search revealed numerous books published by Blandford (many of which dealt with reptiles and birds) that had been included in bibliographies compiled by reputable organizations **(see Figure 3.9).** This reassured her that the publisher was credible.

Even if you know that the publishing company is experienced and responsible, you still need to confirm that the author is an authority on the subject (i.e., has the necessary education and credentials). You can verify an author's qualifications by determining which organizations or institutions he or she is affiliated with. Often a brief biography is included in the publication itself. (Refer to *Who's Who in America* or the *Biography Index* if in doubt.) You might also conduct an author search in the online catalog to determine if he or she published other books or articles on the subject.

Determining the credentials of the author is especially important when you are evaluating articles in mainstream periodicals. Even though many reputable news magazines (e.g., *Time, Newsweek, U.S. News and World Report*) provide accurate information, they are usually not the best source of information for academic papers. This is because journalists write most of the articles in these magazines. They conduct research and interview experts, but they usually are not themselves authorities on the subject.

For instance, in her pet turtle research, my student located a newspaper article about how to prevent the spread of salmonella. However, when she did an Internet search of the author's name, she discovered that the reporter usually wrote restaurant and food reviews. The information in the article is probably accurate, but although the author might be an authority on the tastiest turtle soup in town, she is clearly not an expert on bacteriology. This is why you should locate scholarly journals that contain information written and reviewed by experts rather than reporters.

An author search using the online catalog revealed that the library owns 15 books on reptiles authored by Mattison. A subsequent Internet search revealed that he is a zoologist who has also published numerous journal articles and is an acknowledged expert on wildlife.

Who Is the Audience? Just as it is important to determine a publisher's and author's credentials, so too it is necessary to consider the intended audience of a source. In fact, many choices you make in everyday life are governed by this principle. When baby-sitting your four-year-old nephew, you might rent the latest *Rugrats* movie to entertain him; however, if you popped *Rugrats in Paris* into the VCR on a first date, you'd probably soon have a lot more Friday nights free for baby-sitting. When evaluating a source, the key principle here is that the information is not too simple (or too technical) for an educated adult audience.

For instance, the keyword search for *reptiles* AND *pets* produced one text that lists *Juvenile literature* as one of its subject categories **(see Figure 3.10).** Obviously this work was written for children. Once again, the full-display listing found in the online catalog provides clues that enable the astute researcher to eliminate inappropriate sources.

Figure 3.10 The online index clearly indicates that this book was written for children and would be too elementary for a college research project.

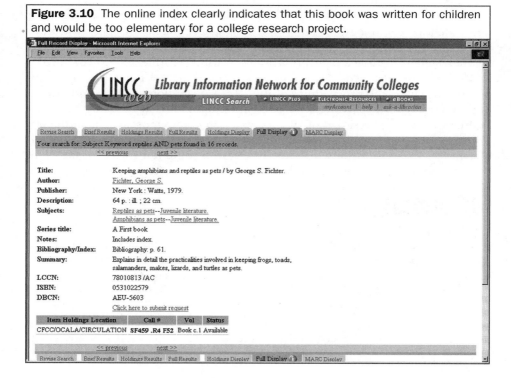

At the same time, you can't rely on receiving such obvious clues in all cases. For that reason, it is important to pay attention to the vocabulary of the source and its attention to detail. Encyclopedia articles generally provide information that is technically correct, but these articles are probably not suitable sources for college-level research papers. This is because encyclopedias target a very general (rather than a scholarly) audience, and they tend to summarize rather than elaborate on a topic.

On the other hand, you also need to eliminate sources that are too technical or specialized. For her "turtle law" project, my student realized she needed to understand more about the transmission and treatment of salmonella. One search uncovered a forty-page article that argued "gram-negative bacteria do not 'secrete' proteins into their environment but only export proteins in their strategic periplasm"[1]. There was no question about the accuracy and academic reliability of this source, but it was so full of medical jargon and technical information that she could hardly read it, much less understand it enough to incorporate it effectively in her own writing.

When Was It Produced? For many research projects, the more up-to-date the information is, the better. Because knowledge is constantly being created and revised, you must carefully note when information was created and determine if it is still valuable. Depending on your topic, you may want to limit your search to information produced in the past five or ten years. If you are interested in some discipline in which information is quickly outdated (such as genetic research), information even a year old may be useless.

On the other hand, because something was produced many years ago doesn't necessarily mean it is irrelevant. Even if your topic deals with a rapidly changing field, such as technology, an older text might be valuable. Suppose you were investigating the history of the development of artificial intelligence; you might be interested in reading a report by Thomas Watson, a former Chairman of IBM. In 1943 Watson declared, "I think there is a world market for maybe five computers." Likewise, the proceedings of the 1977 Convention of the World Future Society might prove pertinent. At this gathering of forward-looking "techies" Kenneth H. Olson, president of DEC (a leader in computer sales that in the 60s produced the first small computer to be sold on a retail basis), announced, "There is no reason for any individual to have a computer in his home." The expectations of these pioneers of the computer industry form a striking contrast

---

ℓ- TIPS

Searching by Publication Date

Many library search tools allow you to limit your search to a particular time period. This allows you to refine your search even further to eliminate inappropriate sources. If your online catalog doesn't have a place in the search window to enter "year" or "publication year," check to see if there is an "advanced search" window that does.

---

[1]Cornelis, Guy R., and Van Gijsegem, Frédérique. "Assembly and function of type III secretory systems." *Annual Review of Microbiology* 54 (2000): 735–74. *Wilson Select Plus.* FirstSearch. Seminole Community College Library. 21 May 2001.

with current attitudes and practices. Depending on your topic, even a text written in another century might prove valuable.

Nonetheless, for many research topics the most current information is the most desirable. For this reason, you need to pay attention to copyright dates. Mattison's book was published in 1992 **(see Figure 3.4).** Because it is almost ten years old, it doesn't offer the most current knowledge on the topic. However, this doesn't mean it won't be a useful source. All the same, this student was cautious about her use of this text and made sure that she located other, more recently published resources to verify some of the scientific information.

What Does It Look Like? It is a well-known fact that the best way to learn to detect counterfeit money is to study the genuine article. Once you become familiar with the appearance, coloring, and texture of real bills, you will immediately spot a false one. For the same reason, starting in an academic library where so much of the information bears the marks of authenticity and reliability will help you recognize suitable sources.

Scholarly work looks serious. By this I mean that it may contain illustrations, graphs, or charts, but it will rarely have glossy, flashy photos designed to appeal to a mass audience. The language used assumes an educated readership. These sources don't "talk down" to the reader; instead, they employ the language used by experts in the field.

Most importantly, a scholarly work offers various forms of corroboration to confirm its credibility. It will support any claims made with statistics and information from other sources. Look for footnotes and parenthetical citations within the text as well as an index, works cited, or bibliography section in the back. Again, the full-text display of the online catalog often will help you determine whether your text has the proper "pedigree" required of a scholarly text. The catalog record of Mattison's book refers to a bibliography and an index **(see Figure 3.11).** The proper documentation of supporting sources is

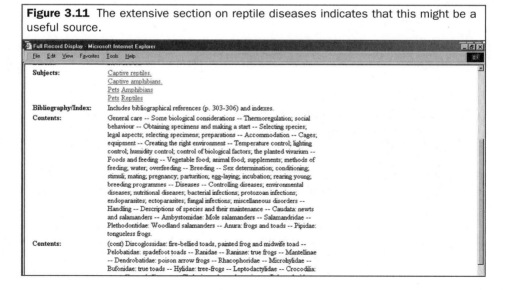

Figure 3.11 The extensive section on reptile diseases indicates that this might be a useful source.

fundamental to academic writing. (You should remember this when you produce your own research project!)

What Do Others Say About It? A recommendation is an important tool in evaluation. When Roger Ebert and Richard Roeper both give an enthusiastic "thumbs up" to a new movie, you are more likely to head to the theater. If a new restaurant gets a positive review in the local newspaper, you might take your significant other there to celebrate his or her birthday. Before buying a DVD player you will probably read what experts have to say about the performance and reliability of various models or brands.

Reviews and recommendations are another way to evaluate the merit of a source. If it has been recommended by an instructor or cited in another reputable source, you can trust that it is credible. Frequently library search tools provide information about the text (a summary, abstract, or listing of the contents) that allows you to better assess whether a resource is appropriate. The full-text display of Mattison's book indicates that there is a bibliography and index. It also contains a very detailed listing of the contents of the book **(see Figure 3.11).**

The Thrill of the Hunt

On most TV detective shows, a crime is committed, a suspect is identified, and the detectives make their arrest—all within an hour. (Sometimes there is even time for the trial and conviction.) In real life, however, the process involves a great deal of mental, as well as physical, "legwork." Some might consider research tedious, but when you begin to gain confidence because you know what you are looking for, where to look for it, and how to properly identify it when you "capture" it, you will begin to experience the "thrill of the hunt."

Exercises

1. Your sociology teacher has assigned a paper on "hate speech on the Internet." Compose a list of research questions that will help you focus this topic and determine the types of information you will need to discover to fulfill this assignment.

2. Access your school's online catalogue, and conduct a *keyword* search (make sure you click on the appropriate "search type") using the phrase *"hate speech"* AND *Internet* (remember to enclose multi-word search terms in quotation marks and capitalize the Boolean "AND"). Choose two of the results that seem most relevant to the assignment, and list of all of the Library of Congress Subject categories that these sources are catalogued under.

3. From the two sources you selected in Exercise 2, choose the one you consider to be the best match for this topic. Using the "Key Factors of Source Evaluation" listed in this chapter, write a paragraph in which you detail why

this source is/is not a credible and appropriate source of information for the assignment mentioned in Exercise 1.

4. Use the passcode provided with this textbook to access the *InfoTrac®* database and conduct a "Keyword" search (check the appropriate term immediately under the search phrase window) for the phrase *"hate speech"* AND *Internet.* Choose the result that appears most relevant. Using the "Key Factors of Source Evaluation" and the suggestions for determining the origins of a source listed in this chapter, write a paragraph in which you detail why this source is/is not a credible and appropriate source of information for the assignment mentioned in Exercise 1.

5. Using the same source you chose in Exercise 4, click on the box marked "Link" in the left margin and a list of related topics will appear. Choose two of these related topics and (in a sentence or two) explain how these topics are pertinent to the assignment outlined in Exercise 1.

CHAPTER FOUR

Get Immediate Results: Databases

> *"As a general rule the most successful man in life is the man who has the best information. "*
>
> **BENJAMIN DISRAELI**

Although I am a bit troubled by his gendered language (Disraeli made his statement in an age less concerned with inclusiveness), for the researcher, his sentiment certainly holds true. Thus, the aim of this chapter is to help you become a successful researcher by showing you how to acquire the best information. Given that we live in "The Information Age," this might not seem to be such a difficult task. After all, as mentioned throughout this book, the Internet has made an enormous amount of information available to anyone with a dial-up or cable connection. But the operative word here is *best*. Note that Disraeli didn't link success to volume: he linked it to quality. The successful researcher is adept at rejecting unreliable and/or unverifiable information in favor of that which is "best"—trustworthy, reliable, and relevant.

For this reason, we initially focused our attention on the library. In fact, until now, the only research tool discussed at length has been the online catalog. Those of you who regularly surf the net may have experienced moments of frustration. You may even have been impatient enough to skip ahead. Compared to the split second access of the Web, the online catalog seems technologically challenged, a tedious, painfully slow way to get what you want. Although the catalog identifies potential sources, you still need to physically find the texts and check them out. If you are accustomed to the immediate gratification of the Internet, the online catalog might seem positively antiquated. Nowadays, if you are reading *Catcher in the Rye* and become curious about what the "J.D." stands for in author J.D. Salinger's name, you can *Ask Jeeves*, <http://www.askjeeves.com>, and get your answer (Jerome David) in seconds. Need to locate the hotel where your friend's wedding reception is taking place? Go to the online yellow pages, type in the hotel name, the city, and state and get not only an address, but also a map to take with you. Stumped about something to cook for dinner? Visit *Betty's Kitchen*, <http://www.bettycrocker.com>, and in minutes choose a recipe that matches the ingredients in your refrigerator. However, there is a library tool that provides immediate access to information in a way that is reminiscent of the World Wide Web. That tool is the full-text database. In fact, students sometimes confuse databases with Web pages because the information they provide is so instantaneous. Databases are likely to be one of the most important resources you'll use as a researcher; through them you can acquire some of the **best** information available on your topic—information you'll need to become a successful researcher.

What Is a Database?

A database, simply put, is a collection of computer data that has been arranged so that it can be automatically retrieved. Computers are great organizers—in fact, you probably have used a computer at home or at work for just this purpose. Businesses usually keep information about customers in a database so they can access it in a number of different ways (according to last name, phone number, address, etc.). When used in reference to library research, however, the term *database* refers to a very specific tool.

Library databases come in two basic varieties: bibliographic and full-text. One way to understand the differences between the two is to consider that all-American institution—*Denny's*. Many of my international students tell me that when they first came to the United States, they frequently ate at *Denny's*. This wasn't because the food reminded them of their native cuisine, but because *Denny's* provides large full-color pictures of the meals in their menu. You don't need to know a great deal of English to order an *Original Grand Slam* from one of these. However, despite the better than real-life photos it offers, no one older than two would confuse the menu with the food itself. Bibliographic databases are like *Denny's* menus. They give you an excellent sense of what a source is like. On the other hand, full-text databases serve up the food, hot and mouthwatering, right to your table. They transmit not only information about a source, but the actual document.

---

e- TIPS

Bibliographic Citations Versus Genuine Documents

The distinction between bibliographic material and the genuine document is important. Sometimes students will cite a bibliographic index or an abstract from a bibliography on their Works Cited pages. I tell my students that is like bringing me a picture from a *Denny's* menu rather than the bacon-cheddar burger and french fries I requested. In order to include a resource in your project, you must track down the actual article.

Bibliographic Databases

A bibliographic database is simply an electronic version of a bibliographic index. You are probably familiar with the bibliographies at the conclusion of a book or article (you even may have been required to include one at the conclusion of a term paper). In these instances, a bibliography is an alphabetical listing of all of the sources a writer has consulted or cited in his or her work. You may not realize, however, that there are many different types of bibliographies. (*The Reader's*

Guide, an index to periodicals that is frequently referred to in high school and public libraries, is one). Although some of these bibliographies are general in nature (they index documents on a broad range of topics), many are devoted to specific disciplines. Print bibliographies, which you will find in the reference section of your library, are typically huge multivolume works with very small type and are usually published annually to catalog all of the documents published that year. To use these hard copy versions, you must look up your key term or phrase in each volume—working year-by-year through the set. The electronic versions are much more user friendly. They allow you to search all of the records (regardless of the year of publication) simultaneously. Be advised, however, that most databases only go back as far as the mid-seventies, some only to the mid-eighties. If you want to locate texts that were published earlier than this, you will usually have to use the printed volumes.

These bibliographic indices operate a lot like the library catalog. They help you discover documents (frequently articles in periodicals, but sometimes government documents, essays, or chapters in books, etc.), but you still need to locate the texts themselves to access this information. Because they are library tools, these bibliographic databases are designed with research in mind: They allow you to locate information according to subject, author, title, or publisher. Often they provide excellent "abstracts," or summaries, of the articles that permit you to evaluate the contents quickly without having to read the entire article **(see Figure 4.1).**

Figure 4.1 This database provides bibliographic information as well as an extensive abstract, or summary, of the article. All of this information can help you evaluate, as well as locate, the text.

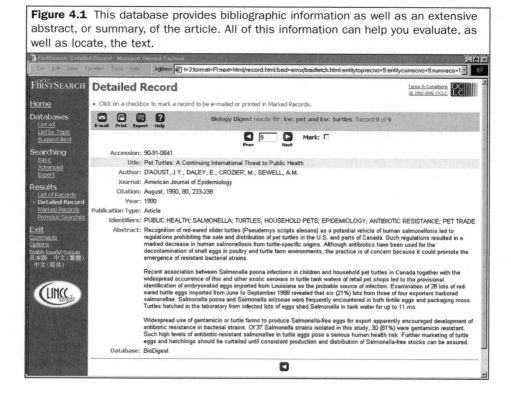

Like their hard-copy cousins, bibliographic databases are usually organized according to specific disciplines or interests. For example, the *Arts & Humanities Citation Index* indexes articles in major arts and humanities journals as well as relevant items from leading science and social science periodicals. *GPO* is an index of U.S. government publications. The *Book Review Digest* provides citations and reviews of current English-language fiction and nonfiction books.

Full-Text Databases

The other type of database is the full-text database. The full-text database is similar in many ways to the bibliographic database. The search mechanism is identical, and it provides a citation as well as an abstract or summary, but (and this is the essential difference) it also delivers the complete document to you, online. This is because full-text databases are actually collections of previously published periodical articles that have been made available in a format that can be transmitted electronically.

Because periodicals are frequently so important to academic research, full-text databases are the most revolutionary of all of the new electronic library tools. Full-text databases provide instantaneous access from one's home or office to numerous newspapers, magazines, and scholarly or professional journals—publications that are published on a daily, weekly, or monthly schedule. You'll recall that periodicals are vital to many research projects for a number of reasons. They are published more quickly than books, so the information in a journal article is often more current than what you will find on your library shelves. Articles that appear in academic and professional journals (as opposed to popular magazines) are frequently written by experts and reviewed by other experts in a field, making them very credible and authoritative sources. They also tend to be more focused than books, rarely exceeding 25 to 30 pages in length. Books, on the other hand, are frequently 200 pages (or more). Although books often provide indices in the back to help pinpoint specific pages for particular facts, you sometimes need to page through a lot of extraneous information to find what you need. In many instances, all you really require is one chapter. If you have limited the scope of your search by posing specific research questions (see Chapter 3), you have a definite idea of what you are looking for. For this reason, it often takes less time to locate what you are looking for in a periodical than in a book.

For those of us who did our undergraduate and graduate work some years ago, the seemingly limitless access to vital research materials provided by full-text databases can evoke a powerful emotional response. Despite years of teaching students to use these tools, I am still amazed by how easy it is to access publications using a database. Although most libraries (public as well as academic) subscribe to major news and popular interest periodicals (e.g., *Newsweek, Time, Sports Illustrated*), until now, only libraries at large universities could afford to subscribe to and house many of the academic journals available. This meant that if you were enrolled at a smaller school with limited holdings, the only way you could acquire an article from some journals was through a lengthy interlibrary loan process that sometimes took four to six weeks. Today, almost all public and school libraries subscribe to numerous databases, some of them full text. As a result, no matter how limited a library's physical resources may be, it can now offer 24-hour access to journals and periodicals that were once available only at major research institutions.

How Do Databases Work?

On-site or Web Site Access

The first thing you need to determine is how to access your library's databases. Libraries pay a lot of money to subscribe to a database, so they almost always limit access to patrons (enrolled students in the case of school libraries or cardholders in the case of public libraries). Some libraries limit access by making the databases available only through on-site terminals (sometimes called intranet connections). This means that you can only use a database if you are in the library or at a related school site (such as a tutoring or media center). Yet, an increasing number of libraries make it possible for students to access a database through a password-protected link to a library Web page or special server. By making databases available via the Internet, these libraries have truly "gone virtual." If you are working on a paper at two in the morning (and many of my students swear they do their best work at that hour) and discover you need an additional source or further information, you can point your browser at your library's Web site and find what you need. You are no longer limited by library hours or physical access, for you can locate full-text academic articles from your home computer.

Systems vary from school to school, so you should contact your library or information technology department if you are unsure how to access your library's database collection. The most important first step is to discover what databases your school has subscribed to and how you can gain access to these important tools. Your library may have published this information on its homepage. Also, with this text you received a subscription to InfoTrac®, a full-text database that is available 24/7 for your research needs.

Search Tips When Using Databases

All of the research strategies we have discussed so far apply to using library databases. Like the online catalog, a full-text database is a "stocked pond." The documents you locate using a database are previously published (and therefore regulated and reviewed) articles. Because it uses an electronic search tool (like the online catalog), a database allows you to "find a perfect match" by using the keywords and phrases you have discovered while converting your topic into research questions (see Chapter 2) and following the leads revealed by your online catalog's subject category hyperlinks (see

Chapter 3). However, understanding a few subtle differences will make your searches more effective.

As mentioned in Chapters 2 and 3, the online catalog uses Library of Congress subject categories for classifying texts. This means that the keywords and phrases that immediately come to mind might not be the most successful search words. (Remember the student who couldn't locate any documents using the search terms *turtles AND salmonella,* but who found excellent resources when she used the terms *reptiles AND pets,* and *"captive reptiles?"*) This is because the online catalog cannot electronically search word-by-word through all of the books on your library's shelves. Instead, when books are catalogued in the library, they are categorized according to established subject headings; you must identify these to access the best information on your topic. Bibliographic databases operate much the same way. When the information about a particular document is entered (such as author, title, publication information), it is also classified with relevant subject categories (often called *descriptors* or *identifiers*) that help you locate the document using a subject or keyword search **(see Figure 4.2).** Be advised that the categories in bibliographic databases are frequently different from Library of Congress terms. Frequently it takes a little trial and error to discover which terms work best.

Figure 4.2 Like the online reference catalog, the "Descriptors" in this database are hyperlinks. If this is a good resource, you might be able to link to other documents that are potential sources.

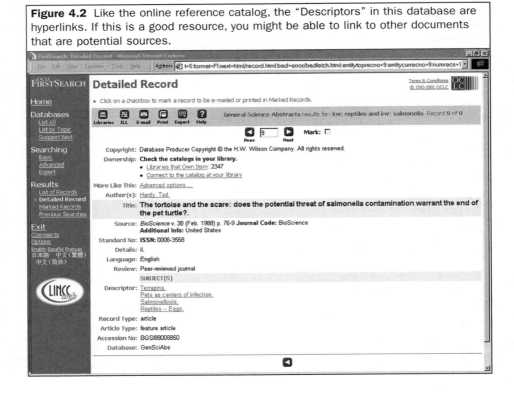

e-TIPS

Keeping a List of Search Terms

Because the search engines of different online tools (e.g., the online catalog, databases, the World Wide Web) respond to different keyword phrases, it is important to keep a list of all possible search terms. Something that is unsuccessful in one system could be produce excellent results in another.

However, because the documents in a full-text database are recorded electronically, database search engines can normally conduct a word-by-word search through each text. This means that a search term that was unsuccessful in the online catalog or a bibliographic database might work in a full-text database **(see Figure 4.3).** A match is made if a keyword appears anywhere in the wording of the document. This may seem fairly simple, but it actually puts a great deal of pressure on you to be precise in how you phrase your searches (and spell your search terms). Remember the tips about multiword and Boolean search phrases (see Chapter 2)? For instance, a full-text database search using the phrase *"school violence"* returned only twenty-four hits (because

Figure 4.3 The search phrase *reptiles AND salmonella* was unsuccessful in the online catalog. However, the search engine of this database was able to locate twelve documents because it searches the entire text—not just subject categories.

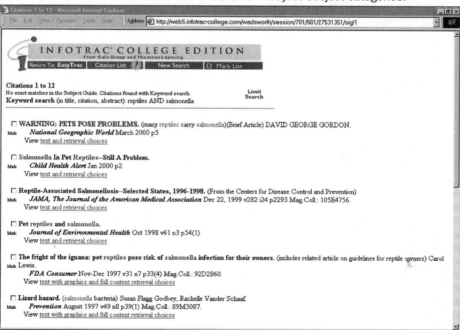

the search engine was looking for the phrase "school violence"). On the other hand, a search using the same tool for *school AND violence* resulted in approximately 3,400 matches. Always refer to the "help" or "advice" links for suggestions on how to best use a database search tool.

ℓ- TIPS

Using Your "Sleuthing" Skills

If you get an overwhelming number of matches for a keyword(s) search in a database, use your "sleuthing" skills. Quickly scan the titles until you locate an article that appears relevant. Read the abstract or summary to confirm your hunch, and if the article proves promising, notice the descriptors or indicators listed. Click on these hyperlinks to locate more articles like the one you have chosen.

Like other electronic library tools, full-text databases enable you to be a "research sleuth," for they provide a way for you to connect with relevant resources (see Chapter 3). Once you locate a promising source, explore these possibilities by clicking on the identifiers or descriptors that hyperlink to lists of other related documents **(see Figure 4.4).**

Figure 4.4 The abstract reveals that this is a pertinent source, and the Descriptor hyperlinks indicate another search phrase (*Reptiles as carriers of infection*) that could lead to more valuable resources.

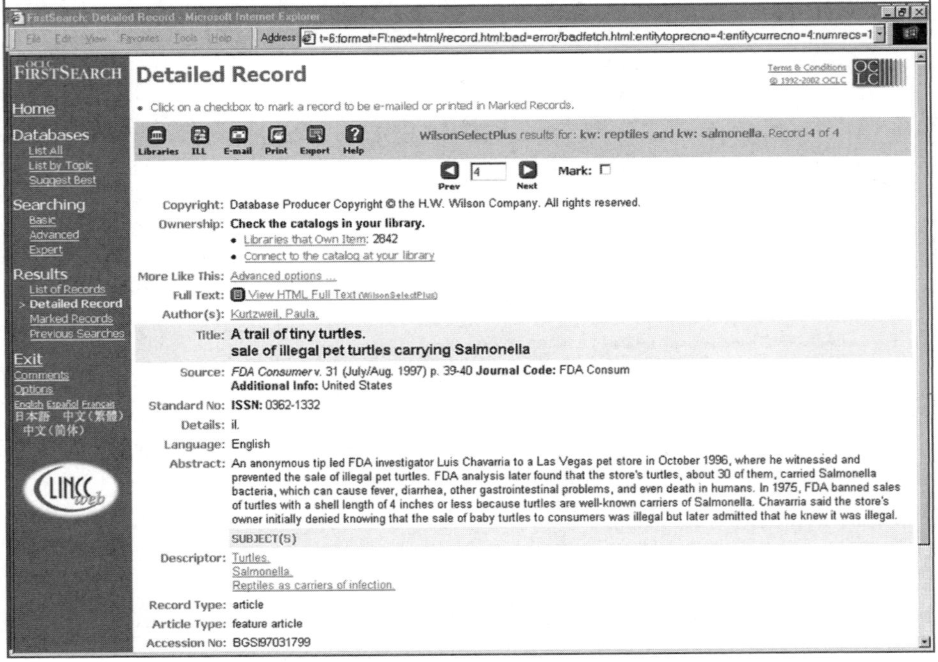

Of course, the beauty of full-text databases is that when you click on the hyperlink to view the "full text," up pops the complete article **(see Figure 4.5)**. You can print it out or read it online. One potential drawback to full-text databases is their limited coverage—most include articles printed only in the last 20–30 years, and none will include every article, however relevant. However, the best databases continue to expand their coverage, increasing their holdings daily.

***e*- TIPS**

Citations for Electronic Documents

The documents contained in a full-text database are reprints of previously published periodical articles that have been reissued digitally. As such, they require a special format for citation that indicates that you accessed them via a database. See Chapters 8 to 10 for more information.

Figure 4.5 A full-text database provides you with a reprint of the complete article, including information about where it was previously published.

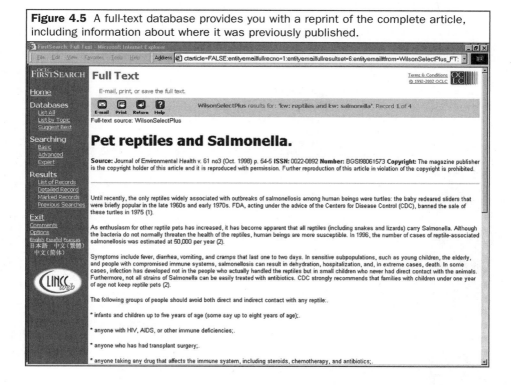

Databases You Should Know and Use

Because libraries make independent decisions about which databases they will purchase, it is impossible to predict what you will encounter at your particular school or public library. However, there are a number of databases that, like the chain stores you encounter in virtually every mall across America (*The Gap, Aeropostale, Structure, Foot Locker, etc.*), are perennial favorites.

Often, libraries will purchase a package deal from a database provider. These are actually database "libraries" that feature numerous databases, some bibliographic, some full text. *InfoTrac®, OCLC FirstSearch, EBSCO Information Services, GaleNet* and *Expanding Lexis-Nexis* are examples of database packages that include databases either singly or in groupings. Deciphering your library's holdings can be a bit confusing at first because some databases can be purchased as either bibliographic or full text. In fact, purchasing a database is a bit like buying a car—there are some things that are standard equipment, but there are a lot of options to choose from as well. For that reason, you might encounter similarly named databases in slightly altered forms in different libraries **(see Figure 4.6).**

If you are attending a large research university, you will probably have access to many full-text databases. At the time of writing, the University of California (Berkeley) subscribed to 40 full-text databases. At smaller schools budgetary considerations often limit the number of full-text databases to which the library can subscribe. In most instances a library will subscribe to one or two general full-text databases (those that offer articles from a broad range of periodicals concerning the sciences, social sciences, and humanities). In addition, it will subscribe to a

Figure 4.6 This is a partial list of the databases Florida community college libraries subscribe to through *FirstSearch*. There are fifty-nine databases, but only five of these are full text (the rest are bibliographic indices). As you can see from the list, many more are available in full-text versions.

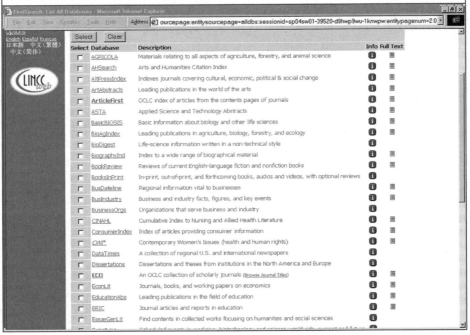

number of more specialized bibliographic databases with indices to articles concerning specific disciplines. If you are fortunate, your library might also offer some specialized full-text databases. Most libraries provide brief descriptions of these databases, you should be able to determine if they are bibliographic or full text. In fact, libraries are not shy about advertising that a database is full text. Usually the phrase "full text" will be prominently featured in the description. If the words *citation* or *abstracts* appear, then it is likely the database is simply bibliographic.

General Full-Text Databases

The following databases in this section are called "general" because they offer articles about a wide range of topics from a broad spectrum of periodicals including many different disciplines and/or mediums (newspapers, magazines, professional journals).

- *Academic Search Elite:* A combination bibliographic/full-text database, it includes full-text articles from approximately 1,500 publications (dating back to 1990) as well as an index to nearly 3,000 additional periodicals (dating back to 1984) **(see Figure 4.7).** Designed with the core curriculum of the undergraduate in mind, this database covers most academic areas of study (e.g., biology, economics, computer science, language, psychology). It

Figure 4.7 Academic Search Premier offers both bibliographic citations as well as full-text articles. Full-text articles are clearly indicated by an icon and the words "full text."

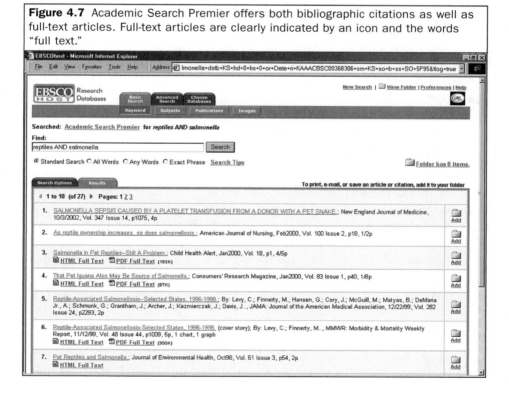

includes more journals devoted to the arts and literature than many other general full-text databases.

- **ECO:** *(OCLC FirstSearch Electric Collections Online)* Combining both bibliographic and full-text entries, *ECO* features over 3,000 publications. One distinctive feature of this database is that full-text articles reprint images or graphics as well as text.

- **InfoTrac®:** This is a huge, user-friendly database that includes over one million full-length articles that cover a broad spectrum of disciplines and topics, dating from 1980 to the present. The database is updated daily and contains articles from both scholarly and popular periodicals including journals, magazines, encyclopedias, and newsletters. The *PowerTrac* search is simple to use and allows you to limit and refine your searches.

- **Lexis-Nexis Academic Universe:** One of the largest databases currently available, *Lexis-Nexis* contains full-text articles on general news, business, law, and medicine from over 6,000 publications (including foreign and domestic newspapers, wire services, radio and television transcripts, and business newsletters, as well as medical, industrial, and legislative journals). Some articles date back 20 years, yet it is updated daily. It is a little bit tricky to use, simply because you must make so many decisions about where you want to search, first in one of the general categories: *News, Business, Legal, Medical,* or *Reference,* and then in one of the many subdivisions, before you can enter your keyword or phrase.

- **ProQuest Research Library:** *ProQuest* contains full-text articles from over 1,000 periodicals as well as bibliographic indexing of another 1,000 titles on a wide range of subject areas. This database allows you to search the entire holdings or limit your search to periodicals in a subject-specific module (e.g., arts, business, education, health, humanities, law, psychology, sciences).

- **SIRSResearcher:** Worldwide sociological, scientific, economic, and political issues are the focus of this full-text database that is indexed according to Library of Congress subject headings. It includes articles from approximately 1,200 domestic and international newspapers, magazines, journals, and government publications from 1988 to the present. Because it includes so many newspapers, there is considerable redundancy (many newspapers pick up the same stories from wire services).

- **WilsonSelect:** This full-text database offers a broad spectrum of articles concerning science, the humanities, and business from approximately 900 U.S. and international professional publications, academic journals, and trade magazines (dating from 1994 to the present). *WilsonSelect's* indexing system is very user friendly, with extensive abstracts and links to other relevant articles. The *Advanced Search* tool is especially helpful if you are looking for a particular article and know the author or the title.

- **WilsonWeb:** Like *Lexis-Nexis, WilsonWeb* is a collection of databases dedicated to various specialties (i.e., applied science, art, business, education, general science, humanities, literature, social science). Articles date from 1995 to the present. Some databases are bibliographic, some are full text, and some are a combination of both. An extensive resource for undergraduates,

WilsonWeb is also user friendly. You can simultaneously search all of the databases or confine your search to one of the specialized databases.

Specialized Full-Text Databases

The following full-text databases limit their selection either by topic (to a specific discipline) or medium (a specific type of periodical).

Business

- *Business Source Premier:* Subjects covered in this full-text database of over 2,000 scholarly business journals include management, economics, finance, accounting, and international business.

- *Business Wire News:* This full-text database provides articles gleaned from national and international business wire services.

Gender/Women's Studies

- *CWI:* (**Contemporary Women's Issues**) This full-text database includes articles from numerous peer-reviewed journals, newsletters, and pamphlets on a broad range of gender-related issues (e.g., violence, health, the military, the media, childcare, human rights) If your topic is in anyway related to gender you should give this database a try.

- *GenderWatch:* A full-text database of current, as well as archival material (in some cases as far back as the 1970s) on subjects that are central to women (e.g., day care, sexual harassment, societal roles) as well as the impact of gender on areas such as the arts, the media, criminology, education, and politics.

Humanities

- *Grove's Dictionary of Art:* An electronic encyclopedia dedicated to the visual arts, *Grove's Dictionary of Art* contains 45,000 articles by approximately 7,000 different scholars on painting, sculpture, graphic arts, architecture, decorative arts, and photography. This database also accesses the Bridgeman Art Library, a digital collection of 100,000 images of painting, sculpture, architecture, and the decorative arts.

- *Literature Resource Center:* A wonderful resource for undergraduates taking a "Writing About Literature" or "Introduction to Literature" course at a school with limited library resources. This database offers online versions of *Contemporary Authors, Contemporary Literary Criticism,* and *Dictionary of Literary Biography,* selected essays from the *Gale, Scribner,* and *Twayne* series of literary criticism, as well as other previously published biographical/critical resources. Search by author, title, or subject, and check out their excellent "webliographies" (guides to select Web sites) on the author search feature.

Law/Government/Politics

- *CQ Weekly Report:* This database provides full-text electronic versions of all articles published in *The Congressional Quarterly Weekly Report* since 1983.

Both citizens and politicians have long considered the *CQ Weekly* an excellent source of nonpartisan information. This database allows you to search its archives by keyword, dates, or subject and features a special "encyclopedia" with entries about all things political.

- **Congressional Universe:** A combination bibliographic and full-text database, *Congressional Universe* incorporates a wide range of legislative and public policy resources including abstracts of congressional publications (some dating as far back as 1789) and full-text electronic reprints of many congressional committee reports and testimony (from 1994 to the present).

Newspapers

- **Ethnic NewsWatch:** With articles from over 200 ethnic, minority, and native press publications, *Ethnic NewsWatch* attempts to offer diverse perspectives and viewpoints. Most articles date from 1990 to the present, but some archival material dates back to the 1980s.

- **InfoTrac® Custom Newspapers:** Libraries subscribing to this database may choose two or more titles from a list of more than 100 newspapers from around the world. Holdings will differ.

- **NewsBank Info Web:** A collection of three specialized newspaper databases: *NewsBank Newsfile* (articles on current issues and events—1991 to the present—from more than 500 North American newspapers) *Business NewsBank* (articles—1993 to the present—from over 400 business journals, newspapers, and wire services), and *Global NewsBank* (articles and transcripts from hundreds of international news sources—1996 to the present—relating to culture, politics, science and technology, etc.)

Reference

- **Biography Resource Center:** An electronic version of *Who's Who*, the *Biography Resource Center* offers encyclopedia like biographies of individuals who have distinguished themselves in the areas of literature, science, multicultural studies, business, entertainment, politics, sports, government, history, current events, and the arts.

- **WorldCat:** When using the WorldCat database, you can limit your search results to Internet resources only. Because it is highly selective, it is an exceptional means to begin exploring the World Wide Web. Sites have already been evaluated with the academic researcher in mind, and it is formatted like other library tools (with source information clearly indicated as well as helpful abstracts and hyperlink subject categories) **(see Figure 4.8).**

Science

- **Earthscape:** A multifaceted database that includes conference proceedings, seminars, and university lectures as well as articles from periodicals and excerpts from books devoted to the earth sciences.

Figure 4.8 When using FirstSearch's WorldCat database, you can limit your results to Internet resources only. This is a good way to find Web sites appropriate for academic research. This search, using the keyword "turtles" returned only 112 matches. A similar search on a commercial search engine could return hundreds of thousands of hits.

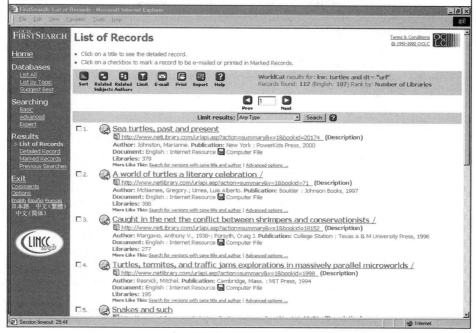

- See also *Applied Science and Technology* and *General Science,* specialized databases included in *WilsonWeb.*

Databases greatly enhance academic research, for they make information of publishable quality available via the Internet for immediate access by anyone with a computer and a modem. If you want to achieve success in your research project, make sure you get the **best** information. Begin with your library's databases before surfing the Web.

Exercises

1. Locate the databases to which your school library subscribes. In a sentence or two, note how many of these databases provide full-text documents, and give the name of one or two general full-text databases that provide access to high-quality sources for a research project. In addition, note the name of a specialized bibliographic or full-text database that relates to your major or your educational interests.

2. Access one of the full-text databases you mentioned in Exercise 1 and conduct a keyword search for the phrase **salmonella AND reptiles.** From the results list, choose the one you consider to be the most credible and appropriate source of information and either print out or copy all of the bibliographic information (author, title of article, original source of publication, copyright date, page numbers) pertaining to it.

3. Because they contain electronic documents, full-text databases can search in a variety of ways, and this can produce different results. Use the passcode provided with this text to access the database *Infotrac®* and click on the *PowerTrac* button near the bottom left of the screen. Activate the pulldown menu in the left box and select "Key Word," then type in the search phrase **salmonella AND reptiles** and click on "search." Write down the number of "hits" you receive. Now clear the search box, and this time select "Text Word" in the pull-down menu and reenter the search phrase **salmonella AND reptiles** and click on "search." Write down the number of "hits" you obtain in this search, and then write a short explanation of why these numbers are different. (Consult the *PowerTrac* "help" link at the top of the screen if you need additional assistance.)

4. Many databases allow you to combine searches to limit your results. Access *InfoTrac's® PowerTrac* (see Exercise 3) and conduct a "Text Word" search for **salmonella and reptiles.** Clear the search boxes and conduct a "Journal Name" search for *Time.* Clear the search boxes, set the pull-down menu on "Select Index (optional)" and in the other window type in **R1 and R2** (this will combine the two search results). Click on "search" and view the results. Give the statistic concerning "salmonella and reptiles" listed in this document.

PART TWO

Research Using the World Wide Web

CHAPTER FIVE

Cast Your Net in Stocked Ponds

"If you put garbage in a computer nothing comes out but garbage. But this garbage, having passed through a very expensive machine, is somehow ennobled and none dare criticize it."

ANONYMOUS

The printed word has a powerful allure. If you doubt this, then the next time you are in line at the grocery store, try *not* to read the headlines of the three or four tabloids that scream for your attention. It is as difficult as driving past a five-car pileup on the interstate without slowing down to sneak a glimpse at the bedlam. Even if you know that tabloids specialize in bizarre half-truths and fabrications, they are difficult to ignore. Not only do we all read these headlines (despite their dubious authority), many of us actually speculate whether there might be some truth to them. Is a certain multimillionaire addicted to painkillers? Could that TV actress be wasting away from anorexia? Might this married movie star actually be gay?

We hesitate to dismiss these trumped-up stories, in part because we have been trained to respect the printed word. Throughout our childhood we are taught to pay attention to books—to read, remember, and repeat what we find in them. Later, we learn that our society recognizes only written documents as legally binding; when we want to attest to the veracity of what we are saying, we "put it in writing." We know, intellectually, that the mere act of writing will not transform a falsehood into a truth. However, when we read a published document, there are powerful dynamics at work that can cause us to accept ideas that we might otherwise reject. These dynamics can, sometimes for good reasons and sometimes for bad, also lead us to think that published opinions and ideas are better than our own.

For this reason, the Internet, in spite of the enormous advances it has made in the transmission of information, can pose many problems for the novice researcher. If the printed word is alluring, then the Internet (with text as well as graphics, moving images, and even sounds) is seductive. Like the tabloids, it can blur the distinction between truth and fiction, between information and entertainment. And, unlike articles published in credible sources, material published on the Web may not have withstood the critical scrutiny of expert review.

Only a decade or so ago, student research was, for the most part, limited to printed media (books, newspapers, periodicals) that were carefully controlled. These controls determined who and what could be published. Today the World Wide Web (WWW) has created a huge grab bag of potential sources. An Internet search might turn up precious sources of information, but it can just as likely lead you to cheap imitations of truth.

Nevertheless, despite its dangers and drawbacks, the WWW does allow access to information that may not be available through your school's library. Throughout this text I have cautioned you to be wary of the Web, yet I spend many of my waking hours online. I use the WWW to locate information that aids me in my professional as well as personal life. To be frank, unless you are attending a large research institution, the WWW might provide you with more current and extensive resources than your school library. If this is the case, the challenge you face is to locate sites from among the millions on the Web that satisfy the rigorous requirements of verification and authentication required in academic research.

Academic Research on the Internet Must Be Authenticated

In everyday life, not all situations require the same level of precision or accuracy. For example, in some circumstances you can vouch for your own identity, whereas for others you are required to offer proof. When you show up for the first day of class, you normally only have to raise your hand or answer, "Here," when the professor calls your name in order to identify yourself. However, when you arrive to take the SAT, you better have two forms of picture ID, or they won't let you sit for the test. In the first situation, you can vouch for yourself; in the second, the College Board demands legal confirmation that you are who you claim to be. Likewise, in most discussions, you can relate information you have read or heard, and (unless you have a reputation as a chronic liar or what you say defies common sense) most people take you at your word. Academic research, on the other hand, has strict rules to establish the reliability of information. You must be able to demonstrate that your information is accurate, indicate where you found it, and demonstrate that the source is credible. Once you grasp the more demanding standards of academic research, you can begin to comprehend— and overcome—the problems presented by the WWW.

Because the standards for authenticating and documenting facts in academic research are much stiffer than those we employ in most everyday situations, library resources generally include only those sources that satisfy these more demanding standards. Online catalogs and subscription databases provide all of the information required to evaluate or verify the authority of a source (**see Figure 5.1**). But unlike your library's digital resources, the Web has no standardized system of organization or categorization. Internet search engines attempt to impose order on this chaos, but each has its own system of classification that affects the outcome of your search. In addition, no one checks the facts on Web pages, so the sites you locate might contain deceptive, biased, or incorrect information. And even when

Figure 5.1 Library resources include most of the specifics you need to assess whether a source is credible and relevant. This entry from a database clearly indicates the author, the publisher, date of publication, and a summary of the information contained in the article.

you locate a resource that is both pertinent and credible, the Web page editor(s) might not include all of the information necessary to adequately document or confirm the source.

For these reasons, it will take all of your research sleuthing skills to locate relevant and reliable sources on the Internet. It is critical that you (1) use search terms that will provide the best matches (see Chapter 2), (2) explore the most promising locations, and (3) evaluate (constantly) the quality of the information you find. The previous chapters have focused on teaching basic research strategies using library tools for the same reason an instructor has a beginning driver practice in the relatively safe confines of an empty parking lot. New drivers need to become comfortable with the equipment and basic skills required before heading out to face the baffling challenges of the highway. Now that you understand basic research skills, you're ready for the unregulated information superhighway.

You might already be adept at navigating the Web. And, if you spend much time on the Internet, you have probably developed your own search strategies and a predisposition for certain search engines. It may seem to you as though you already know enough to negotiate the demands of college research. Perhaps you do. You always need to keep in mind that when you are conducting research for an academic project, you must be *very selective*. When you are using the WWW, you must only cast your net in what I am calling "stocked ponds." Rather than using search tools that rely on computer robot programs to assign matches to your search terms, you need to use search guides that are highly evaluative and will lead you to Web pages that fulfill the sophisticated requirements of academic research.

Academic Research on the Internet Must Be Done in "Stocked Ponds"

As Chapter 2 points out, most Internet search engines compile results by using computer "robots" or "spiders" that rank pages according to algorithmic programs. When you type in a search term, these robots look through the complete text of all of the Web pages in their collection of sites (no search engine currently searches "all" of the WWW) to find pages that include your term. This type of search, which normally doesn't take the context of your term into account, almost always retrieves an unmanageable number of results—and these are not necessarily in the best order for your particular needs.

The most significant difference between regular search engines and subject guides or directories is that the former involve almost no human interaction, whereas the latter rely on a great deal of human selection and evaluation. Given the chaotic nature of the WWW, this assistance in evaluation can be invaluable. *Yahoo!,* one of the most widely used Internet guides, organizes its search mechanism around subject categories. Rather than simply matching terms, *Yahoo!* classifies the Web sites in its pool according to subject headings and returns results based on those headings. In fact, one of the reasons *Yahoo!* has become so popular is because searching by subject, rather than by exact terms, is—in many cases—more successful. When I was looking for the rocking chair for my front porch, I first tried a search engine that strictly relied on matching terms. My search phrase, "rocking chair" returned over 48,000 matches, and most of these pages had nothing to do with purchasing a rocker. In *Yahoo!,* I was able to narrow my quest by choosing *shopping,* then *furniture,* then *outdoor furniture* until I finally refined my search to what I was really looking for. At this point, *Yahoo!* retrieved a mere eleven sites for me to review (**see Figure 5.2).** Although these results are certainly more manageable, this experience illustrates another problem with Internet research: *Yahoo!'s* categories proved ultimately too limiting. Clearly, there are more than eleven online merchants selling teak rocking chairs.

In the most basic sense, *Yahoo!'s* structure is similar to the classification system used in libraries. However, unlike the library, with its standardized Library of Congress subject headings, Internet subject guides adopt their own systems of categorization. *Yahoo!* is an all-purpose subject directory that attempts to address the most common uses of the Internet. It handles communication, everyday questions, and e-commerce rather well because the majority of WWW users are most concerned with these applications. But *Yahoo!* hasn't been designed with academic research specifically in mind. Therefore, its subject headings and Web page selections frequently are not best suited for the topics and disciplines involved in most college-level research projects (**see Figure 5.3).**

Figure 5.2 Using subject categories as a guide enabled me to narrow my search from almost 48,000 hits to 11.

Figure 5.3 This search, using the Boolean phrase "turtles AND salmonella" in the popular search engine *Yahoo!* produced over 4,000 "hits." Reviewing this many Web pages is an impossible task.

Use Search or Subject Directories Most Conducive to Academic Research

There are, however, a number of subject guides that have been expressly designed for academic research. These tools are aptly named "guides" because they steer users to the most appropriate sites and help them avoid inaccurate and/or unverifiable Web pages. Nevertheless, it is important to remember that the same qualities that make these guides so valuable—the fact that they are limited in scope and compiled with a great deal of human evaluation—can sometimes be their greatest liabilities **(see Figure 5.4).** The scope of some guides is limited, is highly specialized, and may reveal the limited perspective of individual human evaluators and compilers.

A subject guide that has been compiled with scholarly research in mind—one that contains Web sites that take a careful and critical approach to academic subjects—is extremely valuable to the researcher who wants to use the Internet to locate resources. Such a guide provides access to a "stocked pond," that is to say, to Web sites that have been appraised and judged current, credible, and relevant because they have been composed by reputable authors or organizations.

⏱ Quick CHECK

Subject Directories and Search Engines Designed for Academic Use

Exceptional Subject Directories:

Librarians' Index to the Internet: <http://www.lii.org/>

Infomine: <http://infomine.ucr.edu/>

Academic Info: <http://www.academicinfo.net/>

BUBL Link 5:15: <http://bubl.ac.uk/link/>

U.C. Berkeley & Internet Resources by Academic Discipline:
    <http://www.lib.berkeley.edu/Collections/acadtarg.html>

Britannica's Best of the Web: <http://www.britannica.com/>

The Internet Public Library: <http://www.ipl.org/ref/RR/>

About.com: <http://www.about.com/>

Suite 101.com: <http://www.suite101.com/>

Effective Search Engines:

AltaVista Advanced: <http://www.altavista.com/sites/search/adv>

Google: <http://www.google.com/>

Alltheweb Advanced: <http://www.alltheweb.com/search?&av=1&c=web>

Moreover, because these guides are designed to be research tools, they often are modeled after library resources. Frequently the subject categories are similar to Library of Congress terms, and (unlike most commercial Internet tools) the initial list produced by a search will include the information necessary to evaluate the relevancy and credibility of a site (e.g., author/creator, date, descriptor hyperlinks, ratings, and a brief summary or abstract of the information). And like an online library catalog, you might need to broaden your search (i.e., search the broader concept or what your topic is about) to locate the distinctive subject categories that will lead you to pages about your topic.

Figure 5.4 This subject guide, *The WWW Virtual Library* <http://www.vlib.org/>, displays a decidedly anti-feminist bias in the results of a search using the term "feminism." Approximately 95 percent of the 143 matches express strong, strident opposition to feminism. It offers a disclaimer that acknowledges this bias, but not all guides will do this.

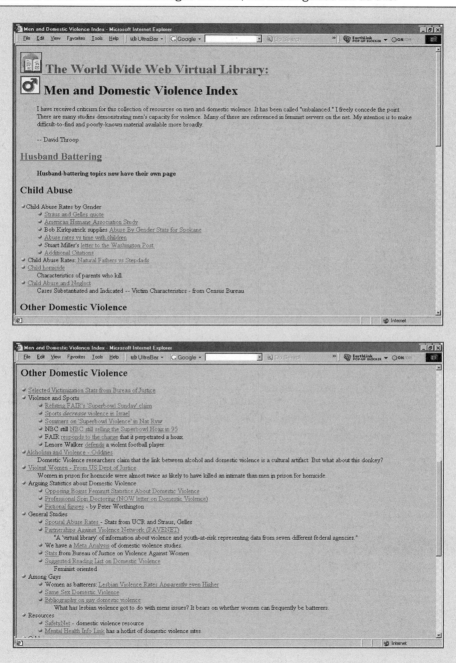

Figure 5.5 This excellent online resource (sources clearly documented) about reptiles was located by following related subject categories in the directory BUBL LINK 5:15. The category *Life Sciences* led to a page with more specialized terms including *reptiles,* which led to this annotated list of reptiles.

The following are some of the best subject guides currently available.

- Librarians' Index to the Internet: <http://www.lii.org/> One of the earliest, most diligently maintained, and well-ordered subject guides on the Internet. It contains over 11,000 quality sites that have been compiled by public librarians. Its scope is limited, but it has been organized to facilitate the academic researcher.

- Infomine: <http://infomine.ucr.edu/> Compiled and maintained by academic librarians from the University of California campuses, this subject guide contains over 31,000 documents that are organized according to university-level subjects/disciplines.

e- TIPS

Learning Search Engine Features

Whether you are using a subject directory or a regular search engine, always take a few moments to familiarize yourself with its features. Make sure the tool recognizes phrase searching (i.e., the use of quotation marks around multiword phrases—"affirmative action"), Boolean terms or has an advanced search mode that enables you to use these methods.

- Academic Info: <http://www.academicinfo.net/> A collection of Internet resources suited for academic research at the undergraduate level and above including links to many full-text resources (online books and journals) under the category "Digital library." This is a good resource, but sparsely annotated.

- BUBL Link 5:15: <http://bubl.ac.uk/link/> Funded by the United Kingdom, this very selective collection of 11,000 Internet sources of mostly academic Web resources is maintained by Strathclyde University in Scotland. Each subtopic area supplies at least five documents for every subtopic, and no more than fifteen (hence the name "5:15").

- U.C. Berkeley & Internet Resources by Academic Discipline: <http://www.lib.berkeley.edu/Collections/acadtarg.html> Maintained by the University of California/Berkeley, this list of Internet resources on many academic disciplines has been selected by subject specialists.

- Britannica's "The Web's Best Sites": <http://www.britannica.com/> Encyclopedia entries are only available to subscribers, but the "The Web's Best Sites" category provides excellent summaries and reviews of Web pages chosen by Britannica editors.

Figure 5.6 This list of returns for a search for *reptiles* in the Librarians' Index to the Internet illustrates all of the benefits of a search guide: a small number of returns (21), information about the author or creator of the site, the date the page was last updated, subject hyperlinks to related topics, and a brief summary of the contents.

- The Internet Public Library: <http://www.ipl.org/ref/RR/>
  The "Reference Center" and "Subject Collections" are limited, but this collection, maintained by the University of Michigan School of Information, is an effort by volunteer librarians and librarian students to provide access to credible academic resources on the Web.

- About.com: <http://www.about.com/> This subject guide can be uneven because each topic is overseen by a different "guide" who determines the content. Some areas are very good, whereas others are disappointingly nonacademic in nature. However, with almost 1 million documents catalogued, it deserves a try.

- Suite 101.com: <http://www.suite101.com/> One of the earliest subject guides constructed by "real" people rather than an educational institution, it is well regulated and has over 40,000 Web documents catalogued in its archives.

Use the Best Commercial Search Engines

It is best to begin with subject guides because they are designed with academic research in mind, and you can be confident that the Web pages you find catalogued in them will be credible. Still, although they are reliable tools, they are not comprehensive. Certainly for some topics (such as ecological threats to the rain forests or critical interpretations of *Moby Dick*) you will find a number of relevant sources. But for topics that are more regional in interest (such as local school bus regulations) or nonacademic in nature (such as waitstaff tipping protocol), you may have difficulty using these directories to locate the information you need.

In the latter case, or to locate additional Web pages on your topic that were not catalogued in the academic subject guides that have just been discussed, you will need to use a search engine. Keep in mind, though, that not all search engines are created equal. Those that are best for shopping or travel (such as *Yahoo!*) are not usually the best for academic research. Here are some of the best search engines currently available for academic research, including some tips on how to use them effectively.

𝓮- TIPS

Learning Advanced Search Engine Features

All of the search engines on the following page (except Google) have advanced search features. In the long run, you will save a great deal of time if you take a few minutes to learn how to use these features to limit your searches. A Boolean phrase in a standard search in most engines is interpreted as a "fuzzy AND" (which means that returns may have just one or both terms included). Most of the advanced search tools permit you to conduct a genuine Boolean search. In addition, these advanced features allow you to specify desired domains (the three letters of the URL that indicate the host address). Because many commercial and personal sites are biased or less credible, specifying domains that are government (gov), educational (edu), or nonprofit (org) can limit your results to more reliable Web sites. Advanced searches can also allow you to limit your results to Web pages that have been updated in the last months or year, thus eliminating "stale" pages that might be out of date. Some even allow you to filter out offensive sites that might give "false" returns because words have been embedded in the page formatting.

- **AltaVista Advanced:** <http://www.altavista.com/sites/search/adv> Perhaps one of the best search engines (because it is so large) for searching for distinctive exact terms or Boolean phrases, *AltaVista* searches the complete text of documents. You must use the "advanced search" feature for Boolean searches; the "sort by" feature makes large lists of returns more manageable.

- **Google:** <http://www.google.com/> One of the biggest search engines, Google employs a unique method of ranking results based on page popularity. A site is given high ranking if a lot of other pages link to it. Sometimes this democratic approach really does result in locating the "best" pages (for instance, when shopping on the Internet), but it doesn't always ensure academic reliability. You will get the best results with *Google* if your search phrase is distinctive and technical.

- **Alltheweb Advanced:** <http://www.alltheweb.com/advanced?&cs=utf-8> Another large search engine, *Alltheweb's* advanced search feature allows you to conduct a variation on Boolean searches ("must include"=AND, "must not include"=NOT) and limit returns or "hits" according to domain (the last terms in the URL that indicate government/gov, education/edu, nonprofit organization/org, commercial/com, etc.).

Figure 5.7 This search, using the advanced mode that eliminated commercial and personal Web pages, and required that the text include "turtles AND salmonella," not include "food poisoning," and be updated in the past three months, narrowed the return list to just under 500 returns.

You may have used a metasearch engine (such as *Dogpile, Copernic,* or *MetaCrawler*) in the past. As the name suggests, a metasearch engine simultaneously searches many search engines to provide a collective list of results. Although this sounds like a time-saver, there are a number of problems with this approach. First, none of the metasearch engines include *Google,* one of the best search engines available for academic research. Second, most metasearch engines ignore quotation marks around multiword phrases and don't recognize Boolean search terms. Finally, none of the metasearch engines have advanced features that enable you to refine your search as you can with *Altavista,* and *Alltheweb.*

Academic Research on the Internet Requires Careful Evaluation

When you locate a Web page that is pertinent to your topic, you will need to evaluate the information carefully, using the criteria described more fully in Chapter 3 (purpose, reputation, intended audience, reliability, and timeliness). Because the WWW is not regulated like a library, the Internet researcher must assume even greater responsibility for conducting background checks to verify that the information on a Web page is correct, credible, and properly documented. As always, the careful researcher is suspicious and never accepts information at face value. In addition to the tips on evaluation given in Chapter 3, asking the following questions about a Web site will help you determine its reliability:

⊕*Quick* CHECK

Evaluate, Evaluate, Evaluate
Academic research on the Internet requires mastery in evaluating the credibility of sources. You must carefully appraise the Web page to determine its
Purpose: *Sarcasm and exaggeration reveal a biased opinion. Does the document present a well-reasoned, balanced approach to the topic?*
Source: *Anonymity destroys credibility. Who is the document written by, and is it affiliated with a reliable organization?*
Intended Audience: *Much on the Internet is designed for general consumption. Does the document acknowledge other sources and treat the topic with a certain amount of complexity?*
Date of Publication: *Good research requires up-to-date information. Has the page been updated regularly?*
Appearance: *You can tell something about a book by its cover. Is the Web site well written and grammatically correct, and does the general layout of the page (graphics, design, etc.) appear scholarly?*
Reputation: *Nothing speaks louder than a good referral. Has the Web site received good reviews or been recommended in a summary or abstract?*

What Is Its Purpose?

Although the Internet was developed primarily to enhance national security, its most common use today is e-commerce. The Internet makes it possible to circulate more information to more people than ever before. It has created a revolution in how goods are advertised, bought, and sold. Because so much on the WWW is intended to persuade you to buy something, it is especially important to evaluate the purpose of a Web site before including the information it contains in your research project. For example, you might think an article entitled "The Benefits of Ritalin" offers an objective analysis of how this drug has helped to treat children with attention deficit hyperactivity disorder (ADHD). However, if it appears on the Web site of the pharmaceutical company that produces the drug, the information will be part of a sales pitch or promotion. Even if a commercial Web page contains accurate information, its undeniable bias makes it of questionable use in a scholarly project.

Where Does It Come From?

Because just about anyone can publish information on the WWW, determining the source of the information on a Web page is especially important. Library sources prominently feature information about publishers and authors; however, on the Internet, authorship and organizational affiliation can be missing, misleading, or difficult to determine.

Be cautious about using an anonymous Web site in an academic research project. Remember that the source of the information you use determines its reliability, so anonymity will make your information suspect. If you know the name of

---

e- TIPS

Verifying the Web Site Author

It is often difficult to determine the author or organization responsible for a Web site (don't confuse a "Webmaster" with the author—a Webmaster may not create the text contained on a page). Look for the following to locate the name of an organization or an author:

- A header, footer, or page watermark that announces the name of an organization. The name of an organization or institution in the URL (this may indicate an official affiliation, but it may not). For instance, a tilde (~) before a name usually indicates a personal site linked to an institutional server. This is not an official page.
- A hyperlink at the bottom, top, or left side of the page to the "home page" (sometimes the link will be labeled "about us") or a hyperlink at bottom of the page to the author's home page.
- A link that allows you to e-mail the organization, the author, or the site Webmaster (you can ask him/her about any affiliations).
- You can also try "backtracking" through the URL by systematically deleting each "layer" or section of the address located between slashes. This might lead you back to the home page.

the organization or author, but have been unable to obtain any additional information, use the search engines *Google* or *Altavista* and conduct a keyword search with the name enclosed in quotation marks. You might also see if he/she is listed at <http://www.whoswho-online.com/> or a site called "Whois" at <http://www. networksolutions.com/cgi-bin/whois/whois>.

On the other hand, Web sites that have been produced by known and respected organizations (whether educational, governmental, or nonprofit) will make excellent sources. In addition, articles in online journals that use peer review by editors or Web pages with articles that have been digitally reprinted from books or journals give evidence of being reliable and truthful.

Who Is the Audience?

When used to support academic research, a source must be more than accurate: the subject it must explore at a level of complexity appropriate for a college assignment. Much information on the Internet is designed for a general, rather than academic, audience. This is because the Internet has become a ready-reference tool for many people. Like the information in an encyclopedia or other general reference, Web pages often provide succinct summaries. Still much of the time, the information you find will be too basic to use as references for a college-level paper, which undoubtedly will require that you go beyond encyclopedia entries in your search for information. (This is why I recommend using a subject guide rather than a commercial search engine—it will direct you to pages that are scholarly as well as accurate.)

Always compare the information you locate on the Web with what you have found using library tools (the online catalog or full-text databases). Because the Internet is so unregulated, Web authors are sometimes careless about acknowledging sources. But like the information found in books in your college library or in articles in scholarly journals, a Web site source can be well researched and documented. Be especially cautious if a site offers numbers or statistics without identifying any sources. An absence of documentation suggests sloppiness, distortion, or worse. One sure indicator of a valid academic resource—on the Web as in your own work—is thorough documentation.

When Was It Produced?

Just as it is often hard to locate the name of the sponsoring organization or author of a Web page, it can sometimes be difficult to determine the date it was created or updated.

ℓ- TIPS

Use "Sleuthing" Skills to Locate Web Authors
Use the same "sleuthing" skills for locating a date of publication as you do for locating the name of a Web author or affiliated organization. Look for a link to a home page or backtrack through the URL by deleting sections of the address.

For many research projects, it is essential that information be up to date to be accurate. As noted previously, knowledge undergoes constant revision, and you want your research to be based on the best information available at the moment. So it is important to note when information was created and determine if it is still relevant. To determine the last update, enter the following: <javascript:alert(document.lastModified)> in the address field and then press <Enter>. The last update information will appear in a window. Be cautious about using information from a Web page that doesn't display a date or bears an old date, especially if it presents information that can change rapidly

What Does It Look Like?

You can often evaluate a Web page by paying attention to the tone, style, or proficiency of the writing. For instance, a pattern of grammatical errors and spelling mistakes are a dead giveaway that a careful, reliable author has not produced the site. Most scholars carefully check their work for these kinds of errors. An occasional mistake in punctuation or spelling is to be expected, but consistent writing errors should raise an alarm.

What Do Others Say about It?

Subject guides often offer brief synopses and reliability ratings. Like the abstracts included in most library resources, these give the researcher a quick impression of the relevancy and validity of a source. Also, confirmation by other sources is important in academic research. Even for topics that are heavily disputed, if an argument is sound, there will be other learned people who agree with it. Beware of radical opinions or ideas that are not substantiated in other places. If you cannot find corroboration, then you should exercise caution in using that information.

To sum up then, the Internet has made innumerable sources available, but they vary in accuracy, reliability and value. Train yourself to recognize a noteworthy resource by familiarizing yourself first with all your library offers on your topic. Then, when you are confident that you know enough to screen out information that is unreliable, unsupported, or poorly argued, venture out into the virtual world of the WWW. Researchers living in the digital age should never settle for unreliable information.

Exercises

1. Since September 11, 2001, there has been a great deal posted on the Internet about terrorism. To get an idea of just how much, go to the *Google* search engine <http://www.google.com> and enter the search term **terrorism.** Note the number of "hits" you get. Next, go to the *Librarians' Index to the Internet* <http://www.lii.org> and record the number of the returns you get using the same search term **(terrorism).** Write a brief analysis that compares and contrasts these two search experiences.

2. Besides supplying information that is of publishable quality, databases also provide suggestions for additional search terms/phrases or ways to refine pre-

vious search attempts that you won't find in most Web search tools. Using the passcode provided with this text, access the database *InfoTrac®* and conduct a "Subject Guide" search using the term **terrorism.** Review the *InfoTrac®* subjects that contain the word "terrorism" (there are two pages of results) and choose three of the phrases that seem particularly interesting or relevant to you. Then access the search engine *Google* <http://www.google.com> and perform searches using these search phrases. In a brief paragraph, compare and contrast the results from these searches with the outcome of the *Google* search you conducted in Exercise 1.

3. The following two sites discuss the controversial issue of racial profiling: <http://www.domelights.com/racprof1.htm>; <http://www.instituteon-raceandpoverty.org/publications/racialprofiling.html>. Write a brief evaluation (using the criteria presented in this chapter and in Chapter 3) analyzing why these Web sites would/would not be credible sources of information for a college research paper on this topic.

4. Now conduct a "Keyword" search in the *InfoTrac®* database using the search phrase **"racial profiling" AND terrorism.** Choose one of the results from this list and write a paragraph in which you compare/contrast the reliability and credibility of this source to the two Web sites in Exercise 3.

CHAPTER SIX

Field Research Online

"You can tell whether a man is clever by his answers. You can tell whether a man is wise by his questions."

MAHFOUZ NAGUIB

For most topics, you will find all of the information you need to write your paper in books, reference works, and databases and on the Internet. For others, you may need to conduct interviews with people who have expertise in the area or to develop a survey that will enable you to understand the opinions of a particular population or group. When you interview or survey people to obtain their opinions, you are conducting fieldwork. Just as the value of any written source must be evaluated according to specific criteria (i.e., whether the source is up to date, pertinent, credible, and reasonably unbiased), so, too, is the value of fieldwork tied to how careful you are in choosing whom and how to query.

Conducting an Interview

Conducting an interview with an expert can make your research project more authentic; it can also give you an unexpected boost of interest or clarity of direction. Speaking to someone who has had firsthand or extensive experience with your topic is exciting. That excitement will often infuse your writing, making it more interesting for the reader as well. Of course, interviews alone can never replace the other forms of research we have already discussed in the first five chapters of this book. Don't assume that an expert will do your research for you or that speaking with an expert will substitute for thorough research. You will still need to conduct library research using the online catalog, databases, and select subject guides on the Internet. An interview is simply one more source of information.

Contact an Authority on Your Topic

The first question to consider when planning an interview is "Who?" As a student at a college or university, you have immediate access to experts in a wide range of fields. My former student who researched the turtle/salmonella law was able to interview a biology professor who had special training in herpetology and a nursing instructor who gave her firsthand information about the medical treatment of salmonella infection. As a citizen, you have access to local, and perhaps even

⊙*Quick* CHECK

Strategies for Locating an "Expert"

- *Consider your campus first:* Professors at your college are an excellent source of information, and they are usually willing to be interviewed for school projects.
- *Approach local officials and agencies:* Part of being a public servant is answering the public's questions. For example, government officials, police, fire, school, and hospital administrators (among others) in your community will often agree to meet with you.
- *Search the phone book:* Many organizations have toll-free numbers. Explore http://www.inter800.com/ for contact numbers of experts on your topic.
- *E-mail a noted expert:* Have you found a Web site with excellent information? See if there is a link that allows you to e-mail the author your questions.

national, government officials. Another student who was investigating the county school and bus scheduling system was able to interview the chair of the local school board. And as a member of the virtual community made possible by the World Wide Web, you have access to countless experts worldwide. A former student interested in the inequities of the financial aid system for nontraditional students was able to e-mail a state official with questions about student loan policies and received answers to his questions within a few days. The Information Superhighway gives you immediate access to innumerable experts who can provide vital, direct information about your subject—or point you in the direction of those who can.

If you're lucky, you might already have an expert in mind that you would like to interview, but most times you will need to find someone who is an authority on your topic. One obvious source is the telephone book or an online telephone directory. Are you investigating the practices of day care providers? Consider contacting local day care centers. Are you examining stalking laws? Check an online "800" number phone book <http://www.inter800.com/> for the toll-free telephone numbers of specific associations that assist victims of domestic violence or sexual harassment. You might feel apprehensive about calling someone you don't know for an interview. However, most people welcome the opportunity to discuss their work, either in person, by phone, or by e-mail. It's a good idea to suggest these different options because some people are more comfortable with e-mail or find it easier to fit an e-mail interview into their schedule. Be sure to call for an interview a few weeks in advance. Before you call, write out exactly why you want to speak to the person and what information you hope to obtain. Be as specific as you can about your research project, and be prepared to explain or give further details if necessary. If you sound knowledgeable and focused, the person you call will be more likely to agree to an interview.

Don't overlook the possibility of tracking down experts through the Internet. Many organizations have Web pages with links that allow you to e-mail questions. If, during the course of your research, you locate an especially pertinent or noteworthy source published on the Internet, and an e-mail address is provided, then contact the author **(see Figure 6.1).** Make sure that your questions extend beyond the information provided on the Web page. You'll also want to allow enough time for a thoughtful reply; you might check your e-mail many times a day, but you can't expect everyone to respond so quickly.

Figure 6.1 This detail-rich Web site is a tremendous resource for information on school violence: it contains up-to-date statistics, pertinent legislation, current programs available, and a database of abstracts on relevant publications. At the bottom of the page a "contact" link connects to another page with e-mail links and addresses to fifteen experts/agencies.

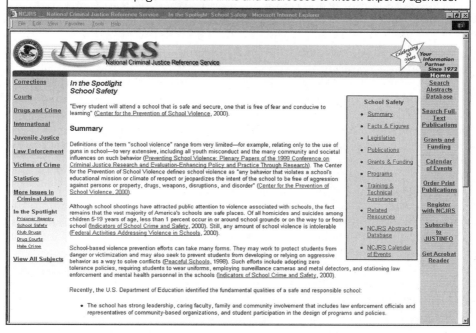

E-mail is an excellent means of carrying out an interview. In fact, even if the authority you are consulting is located on your campus or in your town, you might want to consider conducting the interview via e-mail. There are a number of advantages to this approach. Sometimes it is difficult to coordinate schedules to meet face-to-face; by using e-mail to send your questions and responses, you can avoid this inconvenience. Receiving questions in writing that can be answered after careful consideration, rather than during a personal meeting with time limitations, enables more thoughtful responses. Finally, because you will receive your answers in writing, you will be less likely to forget information or misquote your expert.

e-TIPS

Using Online Discussions as Sources

You might be tempted to use a listserv (sometimes called a mailing group or discussion list) or newgroup (often referred to as a discussion group) to gather personal opinions and ideas about your topic. There are, however, limitations to the usefulness of these forums. The discussions can be an excellent catalyst for stimulating your thinking, but the anonymity that surrounds most of the participants makes this an ineffective means of gathering authoritative information. Most of the people participating in these groups are interested novices, like yourself, rather than experts, and it is difficult to guarantee the credibility of anyone you meet online.

Prepare Your Interview Questions

Once you have located an expert you would like to interview, take the time to develop good questions. Many novice researchers mistakenly think that once they locate an authority and set up an interview, the hard part is over, but composing thoughtful questions—questions that will elicit interesting responses—is equally demanding. In fact, preparing for an interview is an excellent way to refocus your project because it forces you to rethink the questions with which you began your research.

Avoid general questions that will elicit vague answers. Instead, do your homework. Read up on the topic (and the person you'll be interviewing, if possible), so that you can focus your questions and provide an opportunity for the expert you are interviewing to discuss his or her full range of knowledge. Ask for information that is not readily available from other sources. For instance, the student interested in reptiles asked her biology instructor what steps herpetologists took to protect themselves from exposure to the salmonella bacteria and whether he thought reptiles should be kept as pets. In her interview with a nursing instructor, she asked about the specifics of treating salmonella—what kinds of symptoms the patients suffered, for how long, and what the therapy was like. She also asked if she would allow her children to keep a pet reptile, given the danger of infection.

Here are some additional suggestions to help you prepare for the interview.

- Prepare your questions in writing. Doing so will enable you to get the exact phrasing you want and arrange the questions in a logical order.
- Limit your questions to a few that are very specific. It is better to ask three or four pointed questions than eight ambiguous ones. This is especially true in e-mail interviews. Because your expert needs to type his/her replies, you are more likely to get thorough answers if you keep your questions to a minimum.
- Avoid questions that can be answered with a simple "yes" or "no." Instead, ask who, what, when, where—and especially—how and why questions.
- Develop questions that are primarily interpretive or evaluative (e.g., "What is the biggest danger the salmonella bacteria poses to a patient?"), because they will elicit the most useful and interesting responses.
- Consider ending the interview with a question that leads to new information. For example, you might ask your expert to recommend other people to interview or specific books or articles to read.

The Interview and Follow-up

If you are conducting the interview face-to-face, it is important that you keep an accurate record of any and all answers. No one likes to be misquoted. In fact, because I have been misquoted so frequently, I no longer give face-to-face interviews with our school newspaper staff unless they agree to let me review any quotations they plan to use before the article is published. Here are some suggestions for conducting the interview:

- To ensure accuracy, consider tape recording the interview. If you do, be sure to obtain permission from the person being interviewed in advance.
- Take notes — even if you record the interview. Tape recordings have been known to fail.
- Put quotation marks around any statements in your notes that are direct quotations. Check these with the person being interviewed to make sure you have quoted him or her correctly.
- Be flexible. Sometimes a question will generate a response that inspires a follow-up question that you haven't prepared beforehand. If that happens, don't hesitate to add questions or let the interview take a slightly different direction.
- Before you end the interview, check your notes for accuracy. If, in the course of your conversation, your expert furnished you with explicit details or statistics, confirm them while you're still with the person.
- Immediately following the interview, jot down your impressions and complete any unfinished statements in your notes. Clearly mark information that might be most useful to your project.
- If you need to clarify a point or a quotation, make sure you contact the interviewee. To be courteous, you should follow up the interview by sending a short thank-you to the person you interviewed.

Developing a Survey

If you have ever taken a statistics or methods course in psychology or sociology, you know that there is a science to gathering information. Unless you take time to learn the rules about how to compile a random, accurate sample; unless you compose forthright, revealing questions; and unless you correctly interpret the results, you cannot expect your fieldwork to fulfill the strict specifications of academic research. Informal surveys can be useful as long as you thoroughly describe your procedures and qualify your conclusions. In fact, information gleaned from surveys can sometimes lend an immediacy that can energize your project and your writing.

Composing an Effective Survey

Composing a survey is very different from conducting an interview. Interview questions are like essay questions—they are open-ended and attempt to draw out extended answers. A survey is more like an objective test—the questions should elicit short, yet revealing, responses. The questions should be phrased so people can answer quickly, and the responses must fit a pattern that enables results to be easily compiled and compared. Most questions should be answered as simply as "yes/no," "true/false," or with a ranking scale, say from 1 to 5.

Like an interview, however, your survey questions should reflect your own understanding of the topic. You cannot devise a good survey unless you have already completed a good deal of research and are familiar with the most significant ideas related to your topic. A good survey will enable you to include people's views on specific questions you have already formulated: Are motorcycle helmet laws necessary? Does the college need to provide more student parking? Should talk shows that deal with controversial, adult subjects be aired only after 9 P.M.? You need to understand the purpose of the survey before you can create a series of questions that will help you gather the information necessary to respond to it.

Here are some general suggestions for preparing your survey questions.

- Ask no more than 8 to 10 questions.
- Use clear, concise, and unambiguous language. (Test your questions on friends, and simplify any phrasing they find unclear or confusing.)
- Phrase your questions so they can be answered with a yes/no or true/false response or a range of alternative choices (i.e., strongly disagree, disagree, no opinion, agree, strongly agree). Maintain a consistent response pattern to avoid confusion.
- A survey question may simply gather factual information or ask for opinion. In either case, make sure the question doesn't "lead" the respondent.

  Example:
  — Leading: *Are you dissatisfied with the administration's failure to solve the parking problem on campus?*
  — Revised: *Do you think the administration has responded appropriately to the parking problem on campus?*

- Arrange your questions from easiest to hardest. Doing so allows your respondents a chance to warm up before being asked the most challenging queries.
- Prepare your surveys so they are easy to read and complete. Instructions should be brief and explicit. Limit the amount of writing required—instead, respondents should be able to circle or check responses.
- Don't ask for unnecessary or revealing personal information. The more anonymous the survey is, the more likely you will receive an honest response. (If a person's name, age, sex, religious affiliation, employment status, or race isn't relevant, don't ask. If you need personal information to properly interpret the results, then promise confidentiality and honor your pledge.)

Administering the Survey

Like an interview, whom you ask to answer your questionnaire is important. Determine in advance the nature of your target group, and think about ways to best administer the survey to reach representative members of that group. For example, if you want to know what parents think about an issue, then you need to distribute the survey to people with children. You want a random sampling (which means that you want a fair representation of varying opinions and ideas) that polls a cross section of your target group. Polling only your friends or people who agree with you will obviously skew your results.

Failure to identify effectively your target group accurately or to distribute the survey to them will skew your results. For example, I once served on a committee that met with student government officers to determine students' most pressing concerns for change on campus. They had surveyed a few hundred students who were asked to rank how important certain changes in student services or school policies were to them. Expanding the parking lots, improving the food service, and bringing better entertainment to campus ranked very high. But I was surprised to see that providing child care assistance was ranked last: a large percentage of the students in my classes are single mothers who are struggling to balance parenting with their education. When I asked how the survey had been administered, I realized why the results were so curious: No effort had been made to poll men and women in equal numbers, and most of the surveys had been distributed at school functions (such as athletic and social events) that a busy student/mom would most likely not attend. It was clear to me that the results didn't accurately depict the concerns of our student body because the sampling didn't represent the diversity of our student population.

You should model your methods of survey on the professional model—have a random and broad spectrum of respondents. Here are some general suggestions to help guide you in administering your survey.

- Administer the survey yourself to limit the variables and allow you to describe accurately how the survey was conducted.
- Give yourself enough time to administer the survey and tabulate and interpret the results.
- Keep the number of the sample realistic. You might think that the more questionnaires completed, the better. In reality, you can get an effective outcome from a fairly small number of results, as long as the sampling is random. *Suggestion: It is reasonable to assume that your fellow classmates in a general requirement class (first-year English, math, psychology, history, etc.) represent a cross section of the students taking courses in your college. Of course, if the class meets in the evening or on Saturdays, they may not accurately indicate a random sampling of the student population.*
- Use a standardized form to keep track of answers. (You might choose to administer the survey orally, but you should develop a set answer sheet on which to record responses.)
- Record when, where, and how your survey was conducted.
- Carefully tabulate your results.

C-TIPS

Conducting Surveys via E-mail

Surveys, like personal interviews, can be conducted effectively via e-mail. Abide by the same rules concerning random sampling; (don't just e-mail the survey to your friends or family—you must try for a cross sampling of opinion). Make sure that you specify a date of completion, and be prepared to remind people to return them to you on time.

When you report your results in your essay, present your findings in a manner that will make sense to your readers (i.e., use percentages or ratios). Always describe your methods as well: Indicate the date(s) on which you conducted the survey, where you questioned people, and the procedures you followed. Most importantly, specify the limits of your study. Note the number of people questioned, the general population they represented, and the techniques you used to ensure that this was a random sample.

Personally interviewing an authority on your subject or conducting a survey of opinions on your topic can be a useful research experience. Because people are such a great source of information, these methods can reveal ideas and attitudes not available from other sources. Nevertheless, be careful to qualify any conclusions you draw from this data, and resist overstating the results.

Exercises

1. Your psychology teacher has assigned a research paper project, and you have chosen to write about eating disorders. Compose a list of potential experts (using the suggestions you received in this chapter) whom you might interview to help complete this assignment.

2. Access the following article in the *InfoTrac®* database [Hint: use the *PowerTrac* feature and conduct a title search]:

   Browne, Lorna, and Anthony Curtis. "Eat to live or love to eat? The paradox of eating disorders." *Psychology Review* 7.4 (2001): 20–5.

   Using the information contained in this article (and keeping in mind the suggestions made in this chapter), compose a list of five questions you could ask in an interview with one of the experts you identified in Exercise 1.

3. You decide to prepare a survey of the students at your school about eating disorders. Briefly describe in a paragraph what your target group would be and how you would administer the survey to ensure a random sampling of that group.

4. Access the following article in the *InfoTrac®* database [Hint: use the *PowerTrac* feature and conduct a title search]:

   Kowalski, Kathiann M. "Body image: how do you see yourself? How you feel about your body has a big impact on your health. Learn to like the person you see in the mirror!" *Current Health 2* 29.7 (2003): 29–35.

   Using the information contained in this article (and keeping in mind the suggestions made in this chapter), compose a list of five survey questions you could ask of the group you identified in Exercise 3.

PART THREE

Research Documentation

CHAPTER SEVEN

Documentation: General Rules

> *"The wisdom of the wise and the experience of the ages are perpetuated by quotations."*
>
> **BENJAMIN DISRAELI**

If, like many people, you wait until you've written your paper before composing a Works Cited page, you're probably feeling exhausted. For that reason, it is unfortunate if you leave this very important part of the research project for the last minute. What you probably don't know is that many professors turn to the Works Cited page first, even before they read an essay, to obtain a general impression of the research that underpins the paper. (In fact, I know several instructors who will refuse to grade a paper if there are too many errors on the Works Cited page.) Indeed a research paper is only as good as its sources. If you think about that for a moment, you'll see that it makes sense. After all, what is a reasonable person going to trust more, an argument based on the best available evidence, or one grounded in outdated, obscure, or unreliable information? Moreover, if you haven't accurately formatted this documentation page, it will betray (at best) that you are unfamiliar with academic "protocol," or (at worst) that you don't care about the quality of your work. If you don't care, why should your reader?

Properly documenting a research paper requires that you pay meticulous attention to detail. It requires that you accurately identify the nature of your source and that you distinguish and follow the proper format for citing that source, both in the text and on the Works Cited page. In a pre-electronic library, it was fairly easy to determine the type of source with which you were working. The most common were books, articles in periodicals, articles in reference works (i.e., dictionaries or encyclopedias), government documents, pamphlets, or interviews. With the advent of computers, and then the Internet, new systems of delivery have made this task of identification more difficult. Now information also might be delivered by a CD-ROM, a database, a Web site, an online subscription service, or an e-mail. What makes documentation even more complicated is that, as technology changes, these forms are continuously morphing into new modes of data transmission. This makes it extremely challenging for even the most careful writer to remain up to date on the conventions of documentation.

Nevertheless, because improper documentation can sometimes mean the difference between an A or a B, it is in your best interest to incorporate source material into your research paper correctly. You make a strong impression, either positive or negative, by how carefully you integrate material into your essay, acknowledge your research within the text of the paper, and document your resources on the Works Cited page.

A Few Words About Plagiarism: DON'T DO IT!

Many college students are understandably uncertain about what constitutes plagiarism. Their confusion stems from a number of causes. For one thing, beginning writers often aren't taught to paraphrase properly and/or to acknowledge sources when they begin writing "research" papers in elementary school. Thus, very early on they develop the bad habit of plagiarizing throughout their academic careers—without even knowing it.

Plagiarizers Are Not Born; They're Made

I remember when I wrote my first researched essay—it was on Texas. I consulted the *Encyclopedia Britannica,* carefully copied, word for word, pertinent information from this reference work, and then skillfully wove in some of my own words and phrases. Occasionally I enclosed significant sentences in quotation marks, but there were many direct quotations that I did not indicate as such, and much of the rest of the essay was a thinly disguised facsimile of the encyclopedia article that I (incorrectly) considered a "paraphrase." I made a cover out of construction paper, crayoned a likeness of the Lone Star State on the front, and tied the report together with a piece of brightly colored yarn. When I handed it in to my fourth grade teacher, she praised my efforts and rewarded me with an A+. Many students begin their careers as plagiarizers in just this way.

By the time they reach high school, they have become more ingenious. Instead of relying on an encyclopedia alone, they use a variety of sources. They learn to document correctly the places where they have cited direct quotations. They piece together sentences from various sources, change a phrase here and there, and skillfully disguise thoughts and phrases that are not their own. In order to better conceal their theft, some especially clever students might even borrow heavily from a "secret" source that they don't acknowledge in their bibliography or Works Cited page. I have known a number of students who have become very adept at making these plagiarized reports look like their own writing; in actuality, these papers are what I call "plagiarism quilts"—other people's words and ideas stitched together, more or less seamlessly.

The Truth About Plagiarism

Even if you haven't developed such bad habits, you might still be confused about what constitutes plagiarism. There is a great deal of misinformation about this subject circulating in the halls of academe. I have had students confidently assert that so long as they change at least 10 percent of the words in a sentence, it is no longer considered a direct quote, and there is no need to use quotation marks or document the source. Others believe that they need to attribute a direct quote to a source, but a paraphrase doesn't need to be acknowledged. Sometimes I have received papers with little or no direct quotation, but after every sentence there is a parenthetical citation. This is a sad attempt at making a "plagiarism quilt" legitimate. However, and this is the important point, in spite of the students' efforts at documentation, *these aren't really research papers.* They are the subtly altered words and ideas of others represented as original creations. Too many students define plagiarism only as copying a friend's term paper or downloading a paper off the Internet and submitting it, in total, as their own. The truth is, plagiarism takes many forms.

The Many Faces of Plagiarism

Broadly defined, plagiarism is failing to acknowledge the words or ideas of another, but this failure can occur in a number of different ways and be either deliberate or accidental. I often compare these gradations to the different classifications for murder in our legal system. Someone who walks into a fast-food restaurant with an Uzi and opens fire, killing 16 people, is a murderer. Likewise, a busy truck driver who is unable to stop when traffic suddenly slows and rear-ends a commuter, accidentally killing him, is also a murderer, although the trucker may not be legally guilty to the same degree. Whether students deliberately set out to deceive a professor and pass off someone else's words and ideas as their own, carelessly fail to place quotation marks around another writer's words, or neglect to place the proper citation at the end of a paraphrase, the end result is the same. All of these examples constitute plagiarism—it's just that some are more egregious than others.

The important thing to remember is that *whenever* you incorporate information from someone else's work into your own writing, regardless of whether it is a direct quote, a careful paraphrase, or a brief summary, **you must properly indicate the source.** The one exception to this rule is information that legitimately could be considered common knowledge.

Material is considered common knowledge if it's something most people already know or it's something that could be easily found in a general reference source. For example, Ronald Reagan's birthday (February 6, 1911), the number of stomachs a cow has (four), the capital of Malaysia (Kuala Lampur), or the Aaron Copland composition that includes a Shaker hymn *(Appalachian Spring)* are all examples of common knowledge. Most professors would agree that if you can find the information undocumented in several different sources, it is probably common knowledge.

However, if the information is the intellectual property of another writer— whether that information takes the form of statistical evidence, individual opinion, distinctive analysis, original inquiry, or especially compelling phrasing—you need to document the source. In such cases, you must always enclose exact words or unique phrasing in quotation marks and include a proper in-text citation as well as a corresponding entry on your Works Cited page. If you use the same ideas as your source—even if you paraphrase—then you must acknowledge the original in a parenthetical citation and on the Works Cited page. Your instructor expects that as a member of an academic community, you will respect and uphold these basic rules of academic integrity.

⏱ Quick CHECK

Types of Plagiarism

Students sometimes differentiate between "deliberate" and "accidental" plagiarism. But whether you deliberately set out to plagiarize or accidentally fail to acknowledge a source, it is STILL plagiarism.

- **Deliberate plagiarism** involves copying someone else's words and/or ideas and passing them off as your own. (This could be an entire paper, portions of a paper, or simply copying the language and sentence patterns of another person's work.)
- **Accidental plagiarism** involves failing to place quotation marks around another writer's words (even if you provide a source at the end of your essay) and failing to provide the proper citation when you rely on another person's ideas.

A Sure Way to Impress: Incorporate and Document with Skill

As I mentioned at the beginning of this chapter, how you handle research sources in your paper makes a powerful impact. The most significant reason for using direct quotations or paraphrasing is to provide support for your claims or add credibility to your writing. If you let this principle guide you, you will develop expertise as a writer. But it is not enough to avoid plagiarizing; if you want to incorporate information into your project effectively, you must manage your sources skillfully and accurately.

General Rules for Incorporating Direct Quotations

One error that betrays many novice writers is that their essays are too dependent on direct quotations. This error can be manifested in two ways, but both create the impression that the writer lacks confidence in his or her thinking or writing. The first mistake is to quote too often. When the bulk of an essay is the words of others, it seems as if the writer of the essay has "disappeared." The second is to allow quotations to make your points rather than citing the words or ideas of others to support your own assertions and opinions. Your words and ideas always should always dominate the essay. Here are some rules of thumb to help you avoid either error.

- **No more than 15 percent of your paper should be direct quotation.** Most of the writing should be your own. Use the words and opinions of others only to support your own points and ideas.

- **Keep quotations short.** Resist the temptation to quote long passages of text, even if it seems remarkable and strikingly worded. Instead, smoothly incorporate fragments of direct quotations into your own sentences, making certain that the sentence structure is correct and makes sense.

- **Clearly identify each quotation.** If the purpose of direct quotation is to lend credibility to your writing, then you should indicate the authority behind the words. Never simply plop quotations into your paper without specifying who is speaking. Instead, use a signal phrase (sometimes called an identifying tag) to set up the quotation properly.

- **Precede and follow quotations with your own commentary.** Don't use a direct quote to *make* your point. Instead, state your idea in your own words, and supplement that with a quotation from an expert.

- **Interweave your sources.** When quotations from the same source are all clustered in one portion of a paper, it can be a clear sign of a "plagiarism quilt." Instead, your paper should blend information from different sources to create your own analysis.

Example:

- *Original source material:*

  In the early 1970s, the FDA banned the distribution and sale of baby turtles with shells 4 inches in length or less after a quarter million infants and small children were diagnosed with having turtle-associated salmonellosis.

  From: "The Fright of the Iguana" by Carol Lewis in the *FDA Consumer.*

  Approximately 93,000 (7%) cases per year of Salmonella infections are attributable to pet reptile or amphibian contact.

  From: "Reptile-Associated Salmonellosis-Selected States, 1996–1998" in *Morbidity & Mortality Weekly Report* by C. Levy et al.

- *Improper Incorporation of Quotations:*

  But has the law banning turtle sales been successful? "In the early 1970s, the FDA banned the distribution and sale of baby turtles with shells 4 inches in length or less after a quarter million infants and small children were diagnosed with having turtle-associated salmonellosis" (Lewis 33). Nonetheless, "approximately 93,000 (7%) cases per year of *Salmonella* infections are attributable to pet reptile or amphibian contact" (Levy 1009).

Note: *The use of a question, rather than a statement, to lead into the quoted information accentuates the tentativeness of the writer. The excessive length of the quotations and the fact that they are not introduced with a signal phrase amplifies this initial impression. Finally, the facts are presented, but there is no attempt to analyze the significance of the statistics.*

- *Quotations Skillfully Incorporated:*

  Carol Lewis states that the sale of baby turtles was prohibited in the seventies when an outbreak of *Salmonella* affected "a quarter million infants and small children" (33). A recent article in *Morbidity & Mortality Weekly Report* notes that more than twenty years later, of all the cases of salmonella reported each year,

"Approximately 93,000 (7%) . . . are attributable to pet reptile or amphibian contact" (Levy et al. 1009). Obviously, the law banning turtle sales has not accomplished its purpose.

Note how an introductory "signal phrase" clearly identifies the source, direct quotation is kept to a minimum, the significance of the research material is indicated, and different sources are combined in the analysis.

General Rules for Paraphrasing

To paraphrase is to rewrite someone else's ideas in your own words. This is a simple concept, but it is extremely difficult to execute. The challenge of paraphrasing is to relate accurately the sense of a text without duplicating the language. Here are some suggestions to help you paraphrase correctly.

- **Write your paraphrase from memory.** It is very difficult to paraphrase without plagiarizing; if you attempt to rephrase something while you are looking at the original, you are almost doomed to failure. Instead, write your paraphrase without consulting the source. Afterwards, compare it to the original and check for accuracy.

- **Indicate any direct quotation.** Any words or phrases that appear in the original source are considered direct quotes. You must enclose those words with quotation marks.

- **Clearly identify your source.** Just like a direct quote, a paraphrase needs to be introduced to indicate the authority of the source. In fact, an introductory, or signal, phrase is even more important because there are no quotation marks to distinguish these ideas from your own.

Remember, whether it is a direct quote or a paraphrase, you must always indicate your source within the text and on a Works Cited page.

Example:

- *Original source material:*
  Roughly 90 percent of the scaly pets are carriers of salmonella bacteria, says Fred Angulo, a medical epidemiologist with the Centers for Disease Control and Prevention. He has collected evidence that human infections are rising sharply with the animals' increasing popularity. Last year, he says, there were as many as 100,000 cases of reptile-related salmonella poisoning in people nationally—up from about 20,000 just five years ago.
  From: "A Reptilian Pet Peeve" by Ingfei Chen and Deborah Franklin in *Health*.

- *Improper Paraphrase:*
  According to Fred Angulo, an epidemiologist with the CDC, approximately nine out of every ten reptilian pets carry the salmonella bacteria. Angulo has conducted a study that proves that infections in humans are increasing as ownership of pet reptiles increases in popularity. He concludes that last year approximately 100,000 cases of *Salmonella* poisoning was traced to reptiles in the U.S.A.—whereas five years ago there were only 80,000 (Chen and Franklin 24).

Note: Even though a signal phrase and parenthetical citation indicate the information comes from another source, the wording and structure of the passage is too similar to the original, and there are words and phrases that are identical. This would be considered plagiarism.

- *Proper Paraphrase:*
  An article in *Health* magazine reports that recent studies by the CDC link increases in salmonella infections in humans to the growing trend of owning reptiles as pets. Epidemiologist Fred Angulo contends that "roughly 90 percent" of these reptile pets are hosts of the bacteria, and they have caused an 80 percent increase in salmonella infections in the previous five years (Chen and Franklin 24).

Note: The source is clearly identified in the signal phrase, the main ideas are summarized in unique wording and sentence structure, and where exact wording from the original is used, it appears in quotation marks. The paraphrase ends with a properly formatted parenthetical citation.

General Rules for Citing Sources

Any time you directly quote or paraphrase a source, you must provide the information necessary for a reader to locate easily that document and the specific information you have just cited. Students sometimes complain that the rules concerning documentation are too difficult and arbitrary. Indeed, for both the in-text and Works Cited page documentation, there are strict rules about what information to include, in what order it should be given, and how it is to be punctuated. Although many students seem baffled by these rules, the reason for this "pickiness" is to reduce confusion by having everyone conform to the same conventions. Documentation rules establish a uniform, universal format so a reader can quickly determine what type of source is being cited and, if desired, track down the text.

e- TIPS

Format Citations as You Write

Many students make the mistake of leaving the task of documentation until after a paper is completely written. Then they must go back and locate all of the places where they have cited information and retrieve the required details to correctly document the source. They may overlook places in their paper where they need to cite their sources, forget where a quotation came from, or misplace the source they used. It is much better to format as you write a paper. Include a parenthetical citation after any direct quotation or paraphrase. Word processing programs make it very easy to keep a current Works Cited page as you work. Even if you are not sure of the format, you can type (or copy and paste, if you are using electronic sources) the necessary information (author(s), editor(s), title, place of publication, publisher, date of publication, page numbers, date of access, etc.) on the last page or keep a separate file with this information.

What many students don't realize until late in their academic careers (sometimes not until graduate school) is that there is a logic to documenting essays. In some ways, their problem is similar to the difficulties many students have who study Organic Chemistry. I once asked a friend of mine who teaches "Organic" why so many seemingly capable students wash out when they take this course. He explained that the course requires students to memorize an enormous amount of seemingly disconnected information before they can discern a pattern. Few students are able to see the interrelatedness of what they are studying until they are well into the semester. With no conceptual grid to help them make sense of the myriad of facts they are attempting to muster, many falter.

The rules for documenting sources can seem like that. When you look at a style handbook, it can appear that there is no rhyme or reason to formatting rules. However, there is method to the madness. The in-text citation directs a reader to the first piece of information listed in the entry on the Works Cited page. Normally, that is the author's last name. (If there is no author listed, then it will cue the reader to the next piece of information listed; that is the title of the work.)

There are two major styles of documentation: The MLA (Modern Language Association) style is commonly used in the humanities; the APA (American Psychological Association) style is usually employed in the social sciences. Although there are some significant differences between these formats, they are similar. Both require the following information.

1. A signal phrase

- usually appears at the beginning of a quotation or paraphrase, but can appear midphrase
- includes the name(s) of the author(s) or the title of the book, article, periodical, or Web site from which the information originates
- can use a variety of "verbs of address," such as

acknowledges	comments	endorses	reasons
adds	compares	grants	refutes
admits	confirms	illustrates	rejects
agrees	contends	implies	reports
argues	declares	insists	responds
asserts	denies	notes	suggests
believes	disputes	observes	thinks
claims	emphasizes	points out	writes

2. A citation

- provides a brief reference to the source document in the text of the essay
- is located inside parentheses and appears in the same paragraph as the information it documents
- normally appears at the end of the sentence that features the information being cited
- may appear in midsentence, especially if information from more than one source appears in the same statement

3. A Works Cited reference

- appears on a Works Cited page at the conclusion of the paper
- includes all of the required bibliographic information

These three components (signal phrase, parenthetical citation, and Works Cited reference) work together; if you exclude one of them, you have compromised the accuracy of your documentation. If the purpose of direct quotation and paraphrase is to lend authority to your essay, then failing to identify the source seriously undercuts your efforts.

Exercises

1. Briefly (in two or three sentences), and in your own words, explain why it is important to include outside sources in a research paper. At some point in this paragraph, correctly incorporate any portion(s) of the text below as a direct quote. Follow the suggestions you received in this chapter to do this successfully.

> Use quotations selectively to add clarity, emphasis, or interest to a research paper, not to pad its length. Overquoting reduces the effectiveness of a paper because it suggests overdependence on other people's ideas. [From page 108 of Perrin, Robert. *Handbook for College Research.* New York: Houghton Mifflin Company, 1997.]

2. Write a proper paraphrase of the paragraph below according to the instructions in this chapter.

> College students appear to judge cheating as a matter of degree, with plagiarism—perhaps sharing work with a friends or lifting a sentence from an Internet page—as relatively minor, according to a 1999 study of beginning psychology students at a public university. The results, reported by G.A.U. Overbey and S.F. Guilding in "Student Perception of Plagiarism and the Evaluation of Assignments," Journal of Excellence In College Teaching 1999(3), found that more than 70 percent of students said they should be able to resubmit a paper prepared for a previous course. Nearly 65 percent said they should have a chance to redo a paper, rather than receive a zero and be referred for additional campus sanctions, if an instructor catches some plagiarism in the work. Only 3 percent thought "plagiarism" should lead to discipline outside the classroom, while 19 percent said that submission of a purchased paper (a more egregious form of plagiarism, but plagiarism nonetheless) should be referred for student affairs action. Forty-one percent said a zero grade is appropriate for fully copied work. But another 30 percent said that students submitting work with some copied materials should get at least 50 percent credit for "effort." [From page 4 of "How Students View Plagiarism: Implications for Student Services." *National On-Campus Report* 30.5 (2002).]

3. Access the following article in the *InfoTrac®* database [Hint: use the *PowerTrac* feature and conduct a title search]:

Petress, Kenneth C. "Academic dishonesty: a plague on our profession." *Education,* 123.3 (2003) 624–27.

Write a brief summary (4–6 sentences) of this essay. If you directly quote, remember to enclose these words in quotation marks.

4. Using your passcode, access the database *InfoTrac®* and conduct a "Keyword" search for the phrase **plagiarism AND college.** Scan the titles and abstracts of the articles that appear on the results page, and then write a brief paragraph (4–5 sentences) that summarizes common themes, attitudes, and viewpoints of these writers.

CHAPTER 8

Documentation: MLA Format

"Any activity becomes creative when the doer cares about doing it right, or doing it better."

JOHN UPDIKE

A system of documentation is a very precise method of telling your reader where you got your ideas and how you know this information is correct. The Modern Language Association (MLA) style of documentation is used in scholarly publications and in the humanities. Unless your professor specifically instructs you to use a different style, you should use the MLA style of documentation in your essays.

MLA In-Text Citations

The format for in-text citations has been designed to identify source material while interrupting the flow of the essay as little as possible. All that the MLA style requires you to include within the text of your essay is the author's last name and the page number on which the information appears. The reader can use this to reference the author's name on the Works Cited page and obtain more complete information (title, publisher, date of publication, etc.) about the source. This seems rather simple, but because there is some variation in how information is circulated, there can be subtle differences in how the in-text citations might appear.

There are two elements to a correct in-text citation—the signal phrase and the parenthetical citation. How you introduce your information determines what appears in the parentheses.

Examples of MLA In-Text Citations

1. A work by one author

- Carol Lewis states that a midseventies outbreak of salmonella affected "a quarter million infants and small children" (33).

- The <u>FDA Consumer</u> notes that a midseventies outbreak of salmonella affected "a quarter million infants and small children" (Lewis 33).

If the author's name occurs in the signal phrase, then only the page number need appear in the parenthetical citation. If the author's name doesn't appear in the signal phrase, it must be included in the parentheses. If there is an editor instead of an author, the editor's last name should appear in the signature phrase or parenthetical citation.

> **WRITING TIP:** It is important to notice how to punctuate in-text citations. The parenthetical citation appears after the closing quotation mark and before the final punctuation. If a quotation is longer than four typed lines (in your essay, not in the original work), indent the passage one inch (on the left, but not on the right), omit quotation marks, and place the final punctuation mark before the parenthetical citation. The left indentation substitutes for the quotation marks that you otherwise would include.

2. A work by two or three authors

- Chen and Franklin contend that "human infections are rising sharply with the animals' [reptiles'] increasing popularity" (24).

- A recent article in <u>Health</u> magazine declares that "human infections are rising sharply with the animals' [reptiles'] increasing popularity" (Chen and Franklin 24).

If there are two or three authors, list all the last names joined by *and* in the signal phrase or the parenthetical citation.

> **WRITING TIP:** Use brackets to indicate any words that are not in the original wording but you have added or modified to clarify meaning or blend the quotation more readily into your sentence structure.

3. A work by four or more authors

- "Approximately 93,000 (7 percent) cases per year of Salmonella infections," <u>Morbidity & Mortality Weekly Report</u> confirms, "are attributable to pet reptile or amphibian contact" (Levy et al. 1009).

If there are four or more authors, include only the first author's name followed by the Latin phrase *et al.* (an abbreviation for *et alli,* which means *and others*).

> **WRITING TIP:** If you are citing many sources, vary where your signal phrase occurs by locating it in the middle of your quotation.

4. A work by an unknown author

Often articles in encyclopedias, newspapers, dictionaries, and magazines do not include the name of the author. In these cases, the title of the article, NOT the title of the encyclopedia, newspaper, dictionary, or magazine, should appear in the in-text citation.

- A recent article in <u>National Geographic World</u> points affected by the bacteria, so they don't show signs tha ("Warning" 5).

- In "Warning: Pets Pose Problems" the author claims, "Pet reptile affected by the bacteria, so they don't show signs that they are it" (5).

If the author's name is not given, then provide the title in the signal phrase or a shortened version of the title in the parenthetical citation.

> **WRITING TIP:** When you omit unnecessary words to shorten your quotation, indicate this change by using an ellipsis (three spaced periods). An ellipsis never appears at the beginning or the end of a quotation—only in the middle.

5. A quotation within a source

- Stephanie Wong, a veterinarian for the Center for Disease Control, insists, "There's no way to tell that a reptile is salmonella-free" (qtd. in "Warning" 5).

If your source has quoted someone else, identify the original speaker or writer in your signal phrase, in the parenthetical citation use the phrase "qtd. in" (quoted in), the author's last name (or title if no author is given), and the page numbers of your source.

6. A work in an anthology
An "anthology" is a collection of essays or works of literature by different authors.
The name of the author of the essay or work (not the editor of the anthology) appears in the signal phrase or parenthetical citation.

- Because Sarty "feels the old fierce pull of blood" he is often times confused about how to react to his father's violent actions (Faulkner 163).

- Faulkner identifies Sarty's uncertain loyalty to his father as "the old fierce pull of blood" (163).

These citations indicate that you are quoting from a section of William Faulkner's short story "Barn Burning." The passage appears on page 163 of an anthology of many literary pieces.

7. A work by a corporate author
The name of the corporate author (or shortened version of the name) appears in the signal phrase or parenthetical citation.

- According to the American Red Cross, "bleach is an effective means of disinfecting areas that have been infected with salmonella microorganisms" (17).

...fecting areas that have been infected with sal-

...a Red Cross 17).

...nerican Red Cross has produced the item
...passage appears on page 17.

...uthor
...n of the title) as well as the author's name
...cal citation.

...Man Is Hard to Find," the grandmother tries to
...their vacation plans (77).

- Shiftlet cons his way into ~~Lucynell~~'s life in Flannery O'Connor's "The Life You Save
  May Be Your Own" (99).

- Both the grandmother (O'Connor, "Good Man" 77) and Shiftlet (O'Connor, "Life"
  99) are manipulative and deceitful.

These citations indicate that you are quoting from two works by Flannery
O'Connor, "A Good Man Is Hard to Find" and "The Life You Save May Be
Your Own."

9. Works by authors with the same last name
Include the first name of the author you are citing in the signal phrase or parenthetical citation. You may choose to mention the author's full name in the
signal phrase.

- Malcom Smith notes that some Indian snakes have developed special ridges in their
  skin to release pheromones while courting (82).

- Hobart M. Smith proposes that the ridges in snakes' skins provide greater friction
  when climbing and moving (112).

- The ridges in snakes' skins may house special glands that release pheromones (M.
  Smith 82) or provide greater friction when climbing and moving (H. M. Smith 112).

These citations indicate that you are quoting from works by authors who share
the same last name.

10. A work in an electronic source

- In 1996, the <u>Wall Street Journal</u> reported on attempts to "develop a disinfectant
  that can be added to turtle bowl water to kill salmonella germs and prevent later
  infections" (Aeppel).

If your source is an electronic document (e.g., Web site, online journal, article from a database, etc.), treat it as you would any print source—indicate the
name of the author (if no author is supplied, give the title or a shortened ver-

sion of the title) in the signal phrase or parenthetical citation. *(If your document includes paragraph numbers [since there are seldom page numbers in electronic documents], then the parenthetical citation should include the author's last name, followed by a comma, the abbreviation "par." and the number. However, don't create your own paragraph numbers. Use this method only if the document comes with an established system of numbered paragraphs.)*

---

e-TIPS

Page Numbers and Electronic Sources

One problem with electronic sources is that they lack page numbers. Don't be deceived by hard-copy printouts of electronic documents. Because printers differ, the page numbers created in a printout cannot be considered accurate. If the author's last name (or the title, when no author is given) appears in the signal phrase, there is nothing to indicate in the parenthetical citation. However, parenthetical citations play an important role because they designate where source information ends and your writing (or information from another source) begins. This is especially true when you are paraphrasing (quotation marks indicate the end of a direct quotation). Therefore, although it isn't a rule of MLA formatting, I advise my students to find an alternative way to introduce their source in the signal phrase so they can include a parenthetical citation that identifies the author.

---

11. An interview or lecture

Include the name of the interviewee or speaker and her/his job title as well as how you gathered the information in the signal phrase.

- When contacted by telephone, Thomas Boyer, author of <u>Essentials of Reptiles: A Guide for Practitioners</u>, noted that pet turtles pose a significant risk because they are "commonly colonized with salmonella and continually excrete it."

MLA Works Cited Entries

At the conclusion of a research paper, you need to include a Works Cited page that lists all of the references used. If your instructor wants you to list all of the sources you read, whether you cited them or not, this list should be entitled "Works Consulted."

Every entry on a Works Cited page includes the same basic information—author (last name, first), title, and publication information. However, the format (arrangement, punctuation, and spacing) differs depending on the type of source you are listing. Most instructors place a high premium on correctly formatting a Works Cited page. If for no other reason, you need to pay special attention to detail so you can produce a Works Cited page that will boost, rather than reduce, your grade.

The following are a few general rules to follow in order to properly format your Works Cited page.

- Begin a new page for your Works Cited list after the last page of your essay, and center your title (Works Cited) one inch from the top of the page.
- Double-space *everything* on the page (between the title and the first entry, within each entry, and between entries).
- Alphabetize the list by the authors' last names. If no author is provided for an entry, alphabetize according to the *first major word* of the title. (Include words like *A, An,* and *The* in the title, but ignore them when alphabetizing.)
- Begin each entry at the left margin. Subsequent lines in that entry should be indented one-half inch.
- Capitalize each word in the titles of articles, books, etc. except for articles (*a, the*), prepositions (*against, of*), coordinating conjunctions (*and, so*), and *to* in an infinitive, unless it is the first word in the title or subtitle.
- Although convention allows you to either underline or italicize titles of books, journals, Web sites, etc., the MLA prefers that you underline for greater clarity. Whatever your decision, make sure you use the same method (underlining or italicizing) consistently throughout your list. Consult your instructor for his or her preference.
- Use quotation marks around the titles of short stories, book chapters, poems, songs, and articles in journals, magazines, and newspapers.
- Skip one space after each period, comma, and colon. (If a period appears after a title in quotation marks, place the period *inside* the quotation mark.)
- In listing the publisher, follow these guidelines:
  - Omit articles (*A, An,* and *The*).
  - Omit business abbreviations (*Co., Corp., Inc.,* and *Ltd.*).
  - Omit descriptive words (*Books, House, Press,* and *Publishers*).
  - When citing a university press, abbreviate *University* and *Press* (Oxford UP; UP of Mississippi; U of Chicago P).
  - If the publisher's name includes the name of one person (W. W. Norton; John Wiley), cite the surname alone (Norton; Wiley).
  - If the publisher's name includes the names of more than one person, cite only the first surname (Harcourt for Harcourt, Brace, Jovanovich; Prentice for Prentice Hall).
- End every entry with a period.

Printed Sources

In order to format your Works Cited page correctly, it is important to identify the type of source that you are documenting. Standard MLA format for print sources (as opposed to electronic documents) has remained virtually unchanged for years and is readily available in numerous print and online sources. You may have a guide to basic MLA format in a writing handbook and there are numerous Web sites to help you determine the proper format for your sources. The following are two of the best.

Purdue Online Writing Lab (OWL) Handout on MLA Style
<http://owl.english.purdue.edu/handouts/research/r_mla.html#Print>

MLA Style Guide: Capital Community College See the menu on the left margin for quick reference: <http://webster.commnet.edu/mla.htm>.

Books:

Obtain all information from the title page (and the reverse side of the title page), not from the cover.

1. Book with One Author or Editor
Basic format:

> Author (*last name, first*), ed. (*if there is an editor instead of an author*) Title.
>
> Edition and/or volume number. (*if there is one*) Place of publication:
>
> Publisher, date of publication.

Always list the city of publication; if the city is unfamiliar (or if it is the name of a city in more than one state), list the state as well, using the two-letter ZIP code abbreviation.

Examples:

> Fudge, Alan F., ed. Laboratory Medicine: Avian and Exotic Pets. Philadelphia:
>
> Saunders, 2000.

> Frye, Frederic L. Biomedical and Surgical Aspects of Captive Reptile Husbandry.
>
> 2nd ed. Malabar, FL: Krieger, 1991.

2. A Book with Two or Three Authors or Editors
Basic format:

> First author or editor, (*last name, first*), subsequent authors or editors, (*first*
>
> *name, first*), eds. (*if there are editors instead of authors*) Title. Edition
>
> and/or volume number. (*if there is one*) Place of publication: Publisher,
>
> date of publication.

Examples:

> Wray C., and A. Wray. Salmonella in Domestic Animals. New York: CABI.
>
> 2000.

> Johnson-Delaney, Kathy A., and Linda R. Harrison, eds. Exotic Companion
>
> Medicine Handbook for Veterinarians. Lake Worth, FL: Wingers, 1996.

3. A Book by More than Three Authors or Editors
Basic format:

> First author or editor, (*last name, first*) et. al., eds. (*if they are editors instead of*
>
> *authors*) Title. Edition and/or volume number. (*if there is one*) Place of
>
> publication: Publisher, date of publication.

Example:

> Garbrisch, Karl, et al. <u>Atlas of Diagnostic Radiology of Exotic Pets: Small</u>
> <u>Mammals, Birds, Reptiles and Amphibians</u>. London: Wolfe, 1991.

4. A Work in an Anthology
Basic format:

> Author of anthologized work. (*last name, first*) "Title of Anthologized
> Work." <u>Title of Anthology</u>. Edition and/or volume number. (*if there
> is one*) Ed. (*meaning "Edited by," not "Editor(s)"*) Editor's name.
> (*first name, first*) Place of publication: Publisher, date of publication.
> Page numbers.

Example:

> Ryan, Kay. "Turtle." <u>Literature: An Introduction to Fiction, Poetry, and</u>
> <u>Drama</u>. 8th ed. Ed. X. J. Kennedy and Dana Gioia. New York: Longman,
> 2002. 874.

5. An Entry in a Reference Book
Basic format:

> Author. (*last name, first*) "Article Title." <u>Reference Work</u>. Edition and/or vol-
> ume number. Place of publication: Publisher, date of publication.

Often a reference work does not include the author of individual entries. If
no name is given, begin with the article title. Do not list editor of the reference work as the author of the entry.

Example:

> Gaffney, Eugene S. "Testudines." <u>McGraw-Hill Encyclopedia of Science and</u>
> <u>Technology</u>. 7th ed. New York: McGraw, 1992.

If articles are arranged alphabetically in the reference work, omit the volume
and page numbers. When citing familiar encyclopedias or dictionaries,
include only the author's name (if given), title of the entry, the title of the
encyclopedia or dictionary, the edition, and the date of publication.

> "Turtle." <u>The New Encyclopedia Britannica</u>. 15th ed. 1987.

Periodicals:

1. Journal Article
Basic format:

> Author. (*last name, first*) "Article Title." <u>Journal Title</u> Volume number. Issue
> number (year of publication): pages.

In a journal with continuous pagination, do not include only the issue number. For a journal in which each issue begins with page 1, add a period and the issue number after the volume number. Except for *May, June,* and *July,* use three-letter abbreviations for the months (*Jan., Mar., Apr.,* and *Sep.*).

In a range of page numbers, provide the second number in full for numbers through ninety-nine (2–7; 19–24; 56–82). For numbers beyond ninety-nine, provide only the last two digits of the second number, except when additional numbers are essential (92–107; 567–82; 567–608; 1709–14; 4668–777).

Example:

(A journal with continuous pagination)

> Meehan, Shannon K. "Swelling Popularity of Reptiles Leads to Increase in
>
> Reptile-Associated Salmonellosis." Journal of the American Veterinary
>
> Medical Association 209 (1996): 531.

(A journal in which each issue begins with page 1)

> Hardy, Tad. "The Tortoise and the Scare." BioScience 38.2 (1988): 76–79.

2. Magazine Article

Basic format:

> Author. (*last name, first*) "Article Title." Magazine Title date of publication:
>
> pages.

For a magazine published monthly or every two months, indicate the month(s) and year. For a magazine published weekly, indicate the day, month (abbreviated), and year. Do NOT include volume and issue numbers for a magazine. If the page numbers of an article are not sequential, indicate the first page the article appears on along with a + sign.

Example:

> Pritchard, Peter. "Tickled about Turtles." Time 28 Feb. 2000: 76–78.

> Williams, Ted. "The Terrible Turtle Trade." Audubon Mar./Apr. 1999: 44+.

3. Newspaper Article

Basic format:

> Author. (*last name, first*) "Article Title." Newspaper title (*leave out any introductory*
>
> *article ["The"]*) date, edition: section pages.

Example:

> Aeppel, Timothy. "Seeking Ways to Rid Turtles of Salmonella." Wall Street
>
> Journal 30 May 1996, late edition: B 3.

Electronic Sources

The Internet has made it possible to transmit information in new ways, and these methods and modes are in a constant state of flux. The challenge confronting the research paper writer in the age of the World Wide Web is that the essential components of a Works Cited reference (author's name, title, publication information) may be missing from electronic documents or may be present in a form that must be converted into something that makes sense in the MLA formatting system. For example, a Web site may not indicate an author (or the author might use an alias). The layout of an online document might make it difficult to distinguish between two or three possible titles, or there might be no title. A URL and the date when a site was last updated might have to replace more standard publication information. Last, but not least, information that has been "reprinted" on the Web might lack complete documentation about the original source.

𝒆- TIPS

Tricks for Finding Citation Information
If some information (the creator of the Web site, when a site was last updated, a sponsoring organization or institution) isn't immediately available on a Web page, you can sometimes locate these facts by clicking on a hyperlink that takes you to a home page (sometimes labeled "About Us"). Also, you can often discover a home page (and more information about the source) by "backtracking." Try deleting the last portions of a URL to get to previous pages. Remember that a reference is only as good as its source. If you cannot locate a credible author or organization, you may not want to include this reference in your research project.

Yet another obstacle to correctly formatting a Works Cited page is identifying the type of source being used. Doctors need to correctly diagnose a disease before they can begin effective treatment, and researchers must pinpoint the type of source they are using if they want to "match" it with the correct MLA format. When it comes to electronic sources, this can be difficult; there are numerous variations with minute, often difficult to distinguish, differences. You should always remember that the dual purpose of documentation is to give credit to the author *and* to enable a reader to find the material cited. Therefore, you need to determine first whether the source is available via the Web (so it has a URL that can be accessed by anyone with a browser), *or* if it is delivered via a computer but available only through a licensing agreement or password (such as a subscription database, subscription service like AOL, or CD-ROM). Works Cited entries in the former category will include a URL, whereas those in the latter group will not.

In addition to distinguishing how a text is delivered via a computer, there are some general rules to follow when using MLA format to document electronic sources on a Works Cited page.

- If the information has appeared previously in print form, include print information with the other (electronic) information necessary to locate the source.

- If a URL is long and must "wrap" onto the next line, DO NOT insert any punctuation (such as a hyphen). Instead, divide the electronic address after a slash ("/").

- Enclose URLs in angle brackets <>.

- URLs should not appear as hyperlinks. Often word processing programs will automatically transform a Web address into a hyperlink. A quick way to change it back to normal type is to click on "Edit" and "undo."

- Occasionally, the last update is not provided on the home page. To determine the last update, enter the following in the address field and then press Enter: <javascript:alert(document.lastModified)>. The last update information will appear in a window.

𝓮- TIPS

Accurate URLs

It is extremely important that the URL is accurate (otherwise the reader cannot access the page). Because URLs are often confusing and difficult to reproduce, it is always a smart idea to copy and paste (rather than try to type them) into your Works Cited entry.

Electronic Documents Available on the Web. The following examples are for documents that are available to anyone with a browser. Complete information is not always available on Web pages, but you should cite as much of the required information as you can reasonably obtain.

1. Single Web Page

A single Web page is complete in itself and is not connected to a larger professional (e.g., corporate, educational, organizational) Web project.

Basic format:

Author, creator, or editor. (*last name, first*) Title of Web site. (*Use a descriptor such as* Home page [*neither underlined nor in quotation marks*] *if there is no title*) Date the site was last updated. Name of any organization or institution associated with the site. Access date <URL>.

Examples:

Fife, Richard, Salmonella and Your Privilege to Keep Reptiles to be Reviewed by the FDA. 3 Mar. 2003. 7 July 2003

<http://personal.riverusers.com/~richardfife/page20.html>.

Power, Tricia. Salmonella in Reptiles and Amphibians. 19 Feb. 2001. 12 Dec.

2001 <http://www.icomm.ca/dragon/salmonella.htm>.

2. Secondary Web Page

A secondary Web page is part of a larger Web project. The page has a title but also features the name of the project as well.

Basic format:

> Author, creator, or editor. (*last name, first*) "Title of Article or Topic of Page."
>
> Title of Web site. Date the site was last updated. Name of any organization
>
> or institution associated with the site. Access date <URL>.

Example:

> Kuhrt, Trudy. "Trachemys Scripta." Animal Diversity Web. 2 May 2001. U of
>
> Michigan Museum of Zoology. 2 Dec. 2001
>
> <http://animaldiversity.ummz.umich.edu/accounts/trachemys/
>
> t._scripta$narrative.html>.

3. Online Journal Article

Basic format for an article that has previously appeared in a print journal and is being "reprinted" online:

> Author. (*last name, first*) "Article Title." Journal Title Volume number. Issue
>
> number (Year of publication): pages. Access date <URL>.

Example:

> Levy, C., et al. "Reptile-Associated Salmonellosis—Selected States, 1996–1998."
>
> Morbidity and Mortality Weekly Report 48 (1999): 1009–13. 12 Dec. 2001
>
> <http://www.cdc.gov/epo/mmwrpreview/mmwrhtml/mm4844a1.htm>.

Basic format for an article that has never been published in print, but appears only in an online publication:

> Author. (*last name, first*) "Article Title." Journal Title Volume number. Issue
>
> number (Year of publication). Access date <URL>.

Example:

> Rosner, Elsie. "Salmonellosis from a Trip to the Zoo." Physician's Weekly 13.39
>
> (1996). 13 Dec. 2001 <http://www.physweekly.com/archive/96/
>
> 10_21_96/cu4.html>.

4. Online Magazine Article

Basic format for an article that has previously appeared in a print magazine and is being "reprinted" online:

Author. (*last name, first*) "Article Title." <u>Magazine Title</u> Day (*if published*

weekly) Month (*abbreviated*) Year: Pages. Access date <URL>.

Example:

Turk, Michelle Pullia. "New Food Rules for Pregnancy." <u>Parents</u> July 2001: 32–33.

13 Dec. 2001 <http://www.parents.com/articles/pregnancy/1186.jsp>.

Basic format for an article that has never been published in print, but appears only in an online publication:

Author. (*last name, first*) "Article Title." <u>Magazine Title</u> Date. Access date <URL>.

Example:

"Is Your Child Safe From Salmonella?" <u>Medscape Health for Consumers</u> Feb.

2000. 13 Dec. 2001 <http://cbshealthwatch.aol.com/cx/

viewarticle/210245>.

5. Online Newspaper Article

Basic format for an article that has previously appeared in a print newspaper and is being "reprinted" online:

Author. (*last name, first*) "Article Title." <u>Newspaper Title</u> Day Month Year,

Edition: pages and section. Access date <URL>.

Example:

Hampson, Rick. "Tiny Turtle Has Friends and Foes." <u>USA Today</u> 30 Apr. 1999,

final ed.: 3A. 13 Dec. 2001 <http://pqasb.pqarchiver.com/USAToday/

tinyturtle.htm>.

Basic format for an article that has never been published in print, but appears only in an online newspaper or newswire:

Author. (*last name, first*) "Article Title." <u>Newspaper or Newswire Title</u> Date of

electronic publication. Access date <URL>.

Example:

Ripley, Austin. "Salmonella and Reptile Pets." <u>Earth Times News Service</u> 17

Sept. 2001. 12 Dec. 2001 <http://earthtimes.org/sep/

healthsalmonellafromsep17_01.htm>.

6. Online Encyclopedia Article

Basic format:

Author. (*last name, first*) "Title of Article." <u>Title of Reference Book</u>. Year of pub-

lication. Sponsoring institution. Access date <URL>.

Example:

> "Salmonellosis." <u>Encyclopedia Britannica</u>. 2003. Encyclopedia Britannica
> Premium Service. 10 Jul. 2003 <http://www.britannica.com/eb/
> article?eu=667947>.

7. Online Government Publication
Basic format:

> Name of the government. Name of the government agency. <u>Title of Publication</u>.
> Publication city: Publisher, Year of publication. Access date <URL>.

Example:

> Utah. Dept. of Health. <u>Reptile-Associated Salmonellosis</u>. Salt Lake City: Bur. of
> Epidem., 2001. 13 Dec. 2001 <http://hlunix.hl.state.ut.us/els/
> epidemiology/epifacts/reptile.html>.

8. Chapter from an Online Book
Basic format:

> Author. (*last name, first*) "Chapter." <u>Book Title</u>. City of publication: Publisher,
> copyright date. Access date. <URL>.

Example:

> King, F. Wayne, and Russell L. Burke, eds. "Checklist of Crocodilians, Tuatara,
> and Turtles." <u>Crocodilian, Tuatara, and Turtle: An Online Taxonomic and
> Geographic Reference</u>. Washington, DC: Assn. of Systematics Collections,
> 1989. 15 Dec. 2001 <http://www.flmnh.ufl.edu/natsci/herpetology/
> turtcroclist/chklst7.htm>.

9. Online Forum Posting
Basic format:

> Author. (*last name, first*) "Title of Document." Online posting. Date of posting.
> Name of forum. Access date <URL>.

Example:

> Peteralbrian. "Treating Parasites without Fecals." Online posting. 23 Apr. 2003.
> The Herpetological Health Forum. 7 Jul. 2003 <http://
> forum.kingsnake.com/health/messages/5960.html>.

Electronic Documents with Restricted Access. *These sources require a subscription or password to access them. Cite as much of the required information as you can reasonably obtain.*

Databases

1. Journal Article from a Database
Basic Format:

> Author. (*last name, first*) "Article Title." Journal Title Volume. Issue (Year of
>
> publication): pages. Name of database. Name of service. Name of library.
>
> (*If accessed via a library system*) Access date URL of service. (*If accessed via*
>
> *personal subscription*)

Example:

> Lewis, Carol. "The Fright of the Iguana." FDA Consumer 31.7 (1997): 33–36.
>
> Academic Search Elite. EBSCOhost. Seminole Community College Lib.
>
> 13 Dec. 2002.

> Lecos, Chris W. "Risky Shell Game: Pet Turtles Can Infect Kids." FDA Consumer
>
> 21.10 (1987): 19–21. InfoTrac College Edition. Gale. 27 Nov. 2003
>
> <www.infotrac-college.com>.

2. Magazine Article from a Database
Basic Format:

> Author. (*last name, first*) "Article Title." Magazine Title Day Month Year: pages.
>
> Name of database. Name of service. Name of library. (*If accessed via a library*
>
> *system*) Access date URL of service. (*If accessed via personal subscription*)

Example:

> Williams, Ted. "The Terrible Turtle Trade." Audubon Mar. 1999: 44+.
>
> SIRSResearcher. FirstSearch. Seminole Community College Lib. 13 Dec. 2003.

> Pritchard, Peter. "Tickled About Turtles." Time 28 Feb. 2000: 76–7. InfoTrac
>
> College Edition. Gale. 27 Nov. 2003 <www.infotrac-college.com>.

3. Newspaper Article from a Database
Basic Format:

> Author. (*last name, first*) "Article Title." Newspaper Title Day Month Year: pages.
>
> Name of database. Name of service. Name of library. (*If accessed via a library*
>
> *system*) Access date URL of service. (*If accessed via personal subscription*)

Example:

> Webb, Tom. "New Weapon Against Salmonella." <u>Philadelphia Inquirer</u> 20 Mar.
>
> 1998: n.p. <u>SIRSResearcher</u>. FirstSearch. Seminole Community College Lib.
>
> 13 Dec. 2002.

If page numbers aren't provided, use "n.p." to indicate the information is unavailable.

> "Resorts Bid to Save Turtles." <u>New Strait's Times</u> 4 July 2001: 17. <u>InfoTrac</u>
>
> <u>College Edition</u>. Gale. 27 Nov. 2003 <www.infotrac-college.com>.

4. Magazine Article from an Online Subscription Service (e.g., AOL)
Basic Format:

> Author. (*last name, first*) "Article Title." <u>Magazine Title</u> Day month year: page.
>
> Name of service. Access date. Keyword: search phrase.

Example:

> Hogan, Dan. "Rage for Reptiles." <u>Current Science</u> 14 Nov. 1997: 8. America
>
> Online. 15 Dec. 2001. Keyword: reptiles AND salmonella.

5. Encyclopedia Article from a CD-ROM
Basic Format:

> Author. (*if given*) "Title of Material Accessed." <u>Title of Encyclopedia</u>. CD-ROM.
>
> Edition or Version. Place of publication: Publisher, Date of publication.

Example:

> "Salmonella." <u>Compton's Interactive Encyclopedia</u>. CD-ROM. Vers. 2000Dlx.
>
> Carlsbad, CA: Compton's NewMedia, 2000.

6. E-Mail Message
Basic Format:

> Sender. "Subject of Message." E-mail to recipient. Message date.

Example:

> Peppers, Janice. "Salmonellosis in turtles." E-mail to Frank Bonner. 10 May 2000.

Sample Research Paper Using MLA Style

The following paper uses MLA documentation style and provides an example of how to correctly incorporate both print and electronic documents into the text and the Works Cited page of a research paper. Annotations are provided to comment on some of the more complicated aspects of documentation.

Midori Sato   Sato   1
Professor Tensen
English 1101
24 November 2002

How Not to Burn the House While

Roasting the Pig

    "If we cannot protect our children from the obscenity on
Web sites, the only solution is to protect them when they use the
Internet," said Ernest Istook, a Republican, who introduced the
Child Protection Act of 1999 in July (qtd. in Flagg). It's a challenge to preserve First Amendment rights while protecting minors
from Web sites with adult content. I believe politicians should not
enact temporary laws that protect minors but limit the First
Amendment. Instead, they should focus on a long-term solution.
Rather than working to regulate the Internet, we should educate
parents about the safeguards available to ensure that their children are protected from what they feel is inappropriate material
on the Internet.

    During the past decade, Congress has struggled with the
increasing problem of adult material being accessed by minors. In
February 1996, Congress passed the Communications Decency
Act (CDA). The CDA made it a crime to use a computer to show
obscene materials to minors. However, the CDA did not solve the
problem. After the CDA was enacted, the battle between those
fighting to protect freedom of speech and those working to censor

---

[Margin notes:]

Indicate an indirect source (someone quoted within your reference work) by the phrase "qtd. in" in the parenthetical citation.

Center title and double-space between title and body of paper.

Vary signal phrase by placing it at the end of a direct quotation.

No page number is used when referring to a one-page source.

Introduce any abbreviations you intend to use by providing the full title the first time.

Sato   2

Web sites with adult content became even more heated. As one

lawyer has pointed out, the primary problem with the CDA is that

it "criminalizes the transmission of far more than obscenity"

(Sobel). Not all Web sites that contain adult content are enter-

tainment Web sites. Kiyoshi Kuromiya operates the Critical Path

AIDS Project Web site. His site includes safe sex information

that uses street language with explicit diagrams to try and reach

teenagers. Under the CDA, this Web site would be censored,

even though it is educational. This is because the proposed CDA

self-rating systems were similar to television or movie ratings in

that they excluded certain Web sites based on specific words

without considering the general subject matter or purpose

(Strossen 156). Other sex education Web sites might also be

censored; however, teenagers need them. It became clear that

while the CDA was intended to protect minors, it restricted

forms of speech that might actually benefit them. For this rea-

son, on June 26, 1997, the U.S. Supreme Court struck down

the CDA as unconstitutional. In his response, Justice Stevens

wrote that the CDA is like "burning the house to roast the pig"

(qtd. in Cate 56).

In an attempt to follow this call for moderation, Congress

passed the Child Online Protection Act (COPA) the following year.

COPA attempted to correct the errors of the CDA by limiting the per-

Because Web pages don't have pagination, all that appears in the parenthetical citation is the author's name.

This information from a Web page is introduced by the author's name, so it doesn't include a parenthetical citation. The signal phrase contains all the information required to locate the entry in the Works Cited page.

This paragraph includes summarized material from two different sources—a government report and a book that offers a historical overview to the act. Both sources are acknowledged with an in-text citation in the appropriate place in the text.

This signal phrase introduces information that has been paraphrased as well as recognizing the authority of the source.

Paraphrase, as well as direct quotation, must be acknowledged by a parenthetical citation.

Limit the amount of direct quotation by smoothly incorporating remarkable or striking phrases into your own sentences.

Sato   3

sons subject to criminal enforcement of the CDA to commercial Web authors. Under COPA, commercial Web authors were subject to daily fines and even jail time for knowingly placing material on the Internet that was harmful to minors (<u>Recommendations</u>). However, like the CDA, the basic premise of COPA was found to be unconsti- tutional, and the law is currently awaiting review by the Supreme Court (Lewis 92). The Supreme Court most likely will follow the deci- sion made concerning the CDA case. In that decision, the majority of the Court argued that the Internet should receive the same level of protection as the print media. In other words, Web site publish- ers are entitled to unfiltered discretion in free speech. The theory behind the Court's reasoning is the age-old argument that the gov- ernment cannot engage in "prior restraint" of speech. What this means is that if government "restricts speech before it happens," people will be afraid to express themselves (Schmidt, Shelley, and Bardes 114). This would be against our democratic principles.

Its deficiencies aside, COPA is an improvement on the CDA. Placing the responsibility on commercial Web sites is the first step in the solution to the problem of children's online access to adult materials. For example, some adult-entertainment Internet sites provide an Age Verification Service (AVS). This only allows access to users with a special ID. Customers pay a $19.95 annual fee for their ID that allows them access to over 58,000

In citations with 2 to 3 authors, list all the names, separated by commas, with *and* between the last two.

The writer has chosen an alternative way to introduce the source in the signal phrase so she can include a parenthetical citation that identifies the author.

Sato   4

The name of the author or creator of this Web page is unknown, so the title (underlined) is placed in the parenthetical citation.

This paragraph, and the one that follows, has no documentation because they represent the student's own ideas.

adult Web sites (<u>CyberAge.com</u>). In a perfect world, all Web sites with adult content would require an AVS service to prevent access by minors. Once a solid foundation of AVS-backed sites is in place, the Internet will become a safer place for children.

A similar type of commercial cooperation has occurred in other media industries. Thanks to the regulation of the FCC, television broadcasts have little problem with adult material. When families watch network television they usually do not have to worry about scenes with explicit adult content. Cable and satellite channels carry adult content programming, but as long as parents do not subscribe to these channels, adult content will not reach minors. Like network television stations, Web site authors should take responsibility for protecting minors.

No matter what regulations are in force, parents should be responsible enough to protect their children by educating them about the Internet. Unfortunately, children often know more about cyberspace than their parents. Nevertheless, parents should know what is on the Internet, especially about the prevalence of Web sites with adult content. Specifically, parents should be aware of how easy it is for a child to accidentally stumble upon inappropriate Web sites; illicit materials are as close as a click of the mouse away from children.

The best way for parents to learn online safety is to go directly to the source. For instance, CyberAngels, the largest

Sato   5

Internet safety organization founded by the Guardian Angels street

organization, provides parents with the Parent's Guide. This is a

beginner's guide to the Internet that can help parents instruct

their children how to:

you must alter
e exact
wording of a
otation in
der to
egrate it into
ur sentence
ucture
operly,
dicate any
ange by
closing it in
ackets.

>   develop a set of rules to govern their behavior online and
>
>   to guide them into safer waters. [These] rules should be
>
>   designed to help them understand proper netiquette, know
>
>   what to expect from others online, how to behave when
>
>   something unexpected occurs and how to protect them-
>
>   selves from getting hurt in cyberspace. (Aftab 4)

A quotation of
more than four
lines should be
indented ten
spaces and
double-spaced,
with no quotation
marks. The paren-
thetical citation is
placed *after* the
end punctuation.

To conclude, the rapid growth of personal computer and

Internet use has challenged the U.S. government to pass laws to

control the Internet. However, these laws have been held unconsti-

tutional by the U.S. Supreme Court, which has given the Internet

as much protection as print media. Therefore, the responsibility to

protect minors lies with their parents. There are a number of ways

parents can protect their children from inappropriate materials on

the Internet. The first thing parents must do is learn about the

Internet and the various safeguards available. Most importantly,

parents must oversee their childrens' journey into cyberspace.

Sato   6

Works Cited

Aftab, Parry. <u>The Parent's Guide to Protecting Your Children in</u>

    <u>Cyberspace</u>. New York: McGraw, 2000.

Cate, Fred H. <u>The Internet and the First Amendment</u>. Bloomington,

    IN: Phi Delta Kappa International. 1998: 15.

<u>CyberAge.com</u>. 25 Aug. 2002. 6 Jan. 2002.

    <http://www.donsworld. com/verify.htm >.

Flagg, Gordon. "Filtering Mandate Introduced in House." <u>American</u>

    <u>Libraries</u> 30.8 (1999): 12. <u>Academic Search Premier</u>.

    EBSCOhost. Seminole Community College Lib. 8 Nov. 2002.

Kuromiya, Kiyoshi. <u>Critical Path AIDS Project</u>. 8 Nov. 2002. 6 Jan.

    2003. <http://www.critpath.org/>.

Lewis, Anne. "There Oughta Be a Law . . . ." <u>FamilyPC</u> Mar. 2000: 92.

<u>Recommendations</u>. 20 Oct. 2000. COPA Commission. 5 Mar.

    2000 <http://www.copacommission.org/

    report/recommendations.shtml>

Schmidt, Steffen W., Mack C. Shelley II, and Barbara A. Bardes.

    <u>American Government and Politics Today</u>. Belmont:

    Wadsworth, 1997.

Sobel, David L. "The Constitutionality of the Communications

    Decency Act: Censorship on the Internet." <u>Journal of</u>

    <u>Technology Law and Policy</u> 1.1 (1996). 3 March 2000

    <http://journal.law.ufl.edu/~techlaw/1/sobel.html>.

Margin notes (left):

Alphabetize your Works Cited list.

The first line of each entry is flush with the left margin. Indent subsequent lines.

If the author's name is not available, begin the entry with the title of the Web page.

This is an online version of a journal article (not a simple Web page), so include previous publication information.

Margin notes (right):

Always double-space everything on your Works Cited page (both within each entry and between each entry)

If a URL is long and must "wrap" onto the next line, divide the electronic address at a slash ("/").

Strossen, Nadine. "Should Pornography on the Internet Be

Regulated?" <u>Mass Media—Opposing Viewpoints</u>. San Diego:

Greenhaven, 1997: 156.

CHAPTER 9

Documentation: APA Format

"A complex system that works is invariably found to have evolved from a simple system that worked. "

JOHN GALL

A system of documentation is a very precise method of telling your reader where you got your ideas and how you know this information is correct. The APA (American Psychological Association) style of documentation is used in many of the social sciences (e.g., anthropology, economics, political science, psychology, sociology). Nevertheless, you should always check with your instructor to make sure which style he or she prefers. The APA style is similar in many ways to the MLA format. Both use the threefold system of signal phrase, parenthetical citation, and reference list entry to indicate a source. However, the APA style emphasizes the date of publication, both in the parenthetical citation and the works cited reference.

APA In-Text Citations

The format for in-text citations has been designed to identify source material while interrupting the flow of the essay as little as possible. APA format follows an author-date method of citation. This means that the author's last name and the year of publication for the source and—for direct quotation only—the page number should appear in the text, separated by commas. If no author is indicated, use an abbreviated version of the title in quotation marks to substitute for the name of the author. The reader can use this in-text information to obtain more complete information (title, publisher, date of publication, etc.) about the source from the reference list at the end of the essay. This seems rather simple, but because there is some variation in how information is circulated, there can be subtle differences in how the in-text citations might appear. There are two elements to correct in-text APA citation—the signal phrase and the parenthetical citation. **How you introduce your information determines what appears in the parentheses.**

Examples of APA In-Text Citations

Some basic rules for in-text citation in the APA style are as follows:

- The *preferred* method for APA style is to include the author's name and the date (in parentheses) in the signal phrase. If you include a direct quote, then follow this with the page number (or other designation) in parentheses: ex. According to Kurtzweil (1997), in the seventies, "15 million baby turtles were sold yearly in the United States" (p. 39).

- Commas should separate each element of the parenthetical citation: ex. (author, year, p. #) or (author, year).

- If you are directly quoting from a specific part of the text, use the appropriate abbreviation to indicate: ex. *page* (p.), *paragraph* (par.), *chapter* (chap.) or *section* (sec.).

- When citing multiple authors in the in-text parenthetical citation, use an ampersand (&) between the final two names listed.

- If you are listing more than one source within the same parenthetical reference (because they appear within the same sentence) list them in alphabetical order.

- Italicize titles in the text of the essay. (The APA style differs from the MLA style on this detail. The MLA style prefers underlining.)

1. *A work by one author*

- Lewis (1997) states that a midseventies outbreak of salmonella affected "a quarter million infants and small children" (p. 33).

- A midseventies outbreak of salmonella affected "a quarter million infants and small children" (Lewis, 1997, p. 33).

If the author's name and the date of the publication occur in the signal phrase, then only the page number need appear in the parenthetical citation. If the author's name doesn't appear in the signal phrase, it must be included in the parentheses. If there is an editor instead of an author, the editor's last name should appear in the signal phrase or parenthetical citation.

> **WRITING TIP:** It is important to notice how to punctuate in-text citations. The parenthetical citation appears after the closing quotation mark and before the final punctuation. If a quotation is longer than four typed lines, indent the passage one-half inch from the left margin, omit quotation marks, and place the final punctuation mark before the parenthetical citation.

2. *A work by two authors*

- Chen and Franklin (1995) contend that "human infections are rising sharply with the animals' [reptiles'] increasing popularity" (p. 24).

- A recent article in *Health* magazine declares that "human infections are rising sharply with the animals' [reptiles'] increasing popularity" (Chen & Franklin, 1995, p. 24).

If there are two authors, join their names by *and* in the signal phrase and an ampersand (&) in the parenthetical citation.

WRITING TIP: Use brackets to indicate any words that are not in the original wording but have been added or modified to clarify meaning or blend more readily into your sentence structure.

3. A work by three to five authors
The first time you mention the source in your essay:

- This study concludes that "livestock are the main reservoir for human salmonellosis in industrialized countries" (Davis, Hancock, & Besser, 1999, p. 804).

Any subsequent mention in your essay:

- (Davis et al., 1999)

Include only the first author's name followed by the Latin phrase *et al.* (an abbreviation for *et ali,* which means *and others*).

4. A work by six or more authors

- (Ezell et al., 2001, p. 1965)

5. A work by a corporate author
If the name of the corporate author is long, abbreviate it after the first reference. First text citation:

- (American Veterinary Medical Association [AMVA], 1996)

Any subsequent mention in your essay:

- (AMVA, 1996)

6. A work by an unknown author
Often articles in encyclopedias, newspapers, dictionaries, and magazines do not include the name of the author. In these cases, the title of the article, NOT the title of the encyclopedia, newspaper, dictionary, or magazine, should appear in the in-text citation.

- A recent article in *National Geographic World* points out, "Pet reptiles . . . aren't affected by the bacteria, so they don't show signs that they are carrying it" ("Warning," 2000, p. 5).

- In "Warning: Pets Pose Problems" (2000) the author claims, "Pet reptiles . . . aren't affected by the bacteria, so they don't show signs that they are carrying it" (p. 5).

If the author's name is not given, give the title in the signal phrase or a shortened version of the title in the parenthetical citation.

> **Writing Tip:** When you omit unnecessary words to shorten your quotation, indicate this change by using an ellipsis (three periods). An ellipsis never appears at the beginning or the end of a quotation—only in the middle.

7. A work in an electronic source

- An article in the *Wall Street Journal* reported on attempts to "develop a disinfectant that can be added to turtle bowl water to kill salmonella germs and prevent later infections" (Aeppel, 1996).

If your source is an electronic document (e.g., a Web site, online journal, or article from a database), treat it as you would any print source—indicate the name of the author (if no author is supplied, give the title or a shortened version of the title) and the date of publication in the signal phrase or parenthetical citation. (If no date is given, insert "n.d." after the author's name.) **Cite e-mails, interviews, e-mail messages, and online forum postings ONLY in the text of your essay, not in the reference list. Include the name of the author or sender and the day, month, and year of the communication.**

- M. Halverson (personal communication, March 9, 2001)

APA Reference List Entries

At the conclusion of a research paper, you need to include a reference list that includes all of the references used. If your instructor wants you to list all of the sources you read, whether you cited them or not, this list is considered a Bibliography.

Every entry on a reference list includes the same basic information—author (last name, first), year of publication, title, and publication information. However, the format (arrangement, punctuation, and spacing) differs depending on the type of source you are listing. Most instructors place a high premium on correctly formatting a reference list, so pay special attention to detail so you can produce a page that will boost, rather than reduce, your grade.

The following are a few *general rules* to follow to properly format your reference list.

- Begin a new page for your reference list after the last page of your essay, and center your title (References) one inch from the top of the page.

- Double-space *everything* on the page (between the title and the first entry, within each entry, and between entries).

- Authors' (or editors') names should always appear last name first. Indicate first and middle initials (if given).

- If the author's name is not available, the title of the article appears first, followed by the date of publication.

- Alphabetize the list by the authors' last names. If no author is provided for an entry, alphabetize according to the *first major word* of the title. (Include words like *A, An,* and *The* in the title, but ignore them when alphabetizing.)

- If you have more than one work by a particular author, order them by publication date, oldest to newest (e.g., a 1991 article would appear before a 1996 article).

- When an author appears both as a sole author and, in another citation, as the first author of a group, list the one-author entries first.

- Each entry must have a hanging indent (i.e., the first line should be flush with the left margin, and subsequent lines must be indented one-half inch).

- For the **titles of books,** italicize and use "sentence-style" capitalization; capitalize only the first word, all proper nouns, and the first word of the subtitle. Example: *Reptile care: An atlas of diseases and treatments.*

- For **titles of magazines and journals,** italicize and use "headline" style capitalization; capitalize the first letter of each important word. Example: *U.S. News & World Report.*

- For the **titles of book *chapters* or magazine and journal *articles*** use "sentence-style" capitalization, and *do not* use underlining, italics, or quotation marks. Example: A trail of tiny turtles.

- For the **publisher's name, omit terms unnecessary to convey your meaning (e.g., *Publishers, Co.,* and *Inc.*).

- Skip one space after each period, comma, and colon. (If a period appears after a title in quotation marks, place the period *inside* the quotation mark.)

- End every entry with a period, except when a URL appears as the last item in the entry.

Printed Sources

In order to correctly format your reference list, it is important to identify the type of source that you are documenting. Standard APA format for print sources (as opposed to electronic documents) has remained virtually unchanged for years and is readily available in numerous print and online sources. You probably have a guide to basic APA format in your textbook, and there are numerous Web sites to help you determine the proper format for your sources. The following are two of the best.

Purdue Online Writing Lab (OWL) Handout on APA Style

<http://owl.english.purdue.edu/handouts/research/r_apa.html>

APA Style Guide: Capital Community College

<http://webster.commnet.edu/apa/apa_index.htm>

Books:

1. Book with One Author or Editor
Basic format:

Author (*last name, first initial*). (Ed.). (*if there is an editor instead of an author*) (year of

publication). *Title.* (volume and/or edition number). (*if there is one*) Place of

publication: Publisher.

Always list the city of publication; if the city is unfamiliar (or if it is the name of a city in more than one state), list the state as well using the two-letter ZIP code abbreviation.
Examples:

Ackerman, L. (Ed.). (1997). *The biology, husbandry and health care of reptiles.* Neptune

City, NJ: T.F.H.

Frye, F. L. (1991). *Biomedical and surgical aspects of captive reptile husbandry* (Vols. 1–2).

Malabar, FL: Krieger.

2. A Book with More than One Author or Editor
Basic format:

Authors. (*last name, first initial, with comma and ampersand before last author*). (Eds.).

(*if there are editors instead of authors*) (year of publication). *Title.* (volume

and/or edition number). (*if there is one*) Place of publication: Publisher.

Examples:

> Bartlett, R. D., & Bartlett, P. P. (1999). *Terrarium and cage construction and care.* Hauppauge, NY: Barron's Educational Series.

> Warwick, C., Frye, F. L., & Murphy, J. B. (Eds.). (1995). *Health and welfare of captive reptiles.* New York: Chapman & Hall.

3. Article in a Reference Book:
Basic format:

> Author. (*last name, first initial*) (year of publication). Article title. In *Book Title* (Vol. #, pp. #'s). Place of publication: Publisher.

Example:

> Rouf, M. A. (1991). Salmonella. In *The encyclopedia of human biology* (Vol. 6, pp. 701–714). New York: Academic Press.

Perodicals:

4. An Article in a Scholarly Journal
Basic format:

> Author. (*last name, first initial*) (year of publication). Article title. *Journal Title, volume number*(issue number), pages.

Example:

> Pasmans, F., De Herdt, P., & Haesebrouck, F. (2002). The presence of salmonella infections in freshwater turtles. *The Veterinary Record, 150*(10), 692–693.

Notice that the journal title and volume number are italicized.

5. An Article in a Magazine
Basic format:

> Author. (*last name, first initial*) (Year, month day). Article title. *Magazine Title,* pages.

Example:

> Adler, T. (1999, November). Turtles in trouble. *National Geographic World,* 17–22.

6. Newspaper Article
Basic format:

> Author. (*last name, first initial*) (Year, month day). Article title. *Name of*
>
> *Newspaper,* pages.

Example:

> Clines, F. X. (2002, August 4). Civil War relics draw visitors, and con artists.
>
> *New York Times,* A12.

> Hampson, R. (1999, April 30). Tiny turtle has friends and foes. *USA Today,* A3.
>
> *If no page numbers are given, indicate this with "n. p."*

Electronic Sources

The Internet has made it possible to transmit information in new ways, and these methods and modes are in a constant state of flux. The challenge confronting the research paper writer in the age of the Internet is that the essential components of a reference list entry (author's name, year of publication, title, publication information) may be missing from electronic documents, or they might be present in a form that must be converted into something that makes sense in the APA formatting system. For example, a Web site may not indicate an author (or the author might use an alias). The layout of an online document might make it difficult to distinguish between two or three possible titles, or there might be no title. A URL and the date when a site was last updated might have to replace more standard publication information. Last, but not least, information that has been "reprinted" on the Web might lack complete documentation about the original source.

Yet another obstacle to correctly formatting a reference list is identifying the type of source being used. Doctors need to correctly diagnose a disease before they can begin effective treatment, and researchers must pinpoint the type of source they are using if they want to "match" it with the correct APA format. When it comes to electronic sources, this can be difficult; there are numerous variations with minute, often difficult to distinguish, differences. You should always remember that the dual purpose of documentation is to give credit to the author *and* to enable a reader to find the material cited. Therefore, you need to determine first whether the source is available via the Web (so it has a URL that can be accessed by anyone with a browser), *or* if it is delivered via a computer but available only through a licensing agreement or password (such as a subscription database, subscription service like AOL, or a CD-ROM). Reference list entries in the former category will include a URL, whereas those in the latter group will not.

> **_e_-TIPS**
>
> ## APA Style for Web Documents
> A special problem confronting anyone who wants to document electronic documents using APA style is that although the association has issued directions concerning previously published texts that have been reprinted online, they have been slow to develop formatting rules for Web documents. In this text I have attempted to use the principles of APA documentation style to extrapolate a format for Web pages that agrees with the official rules of the APA's _Publication Manual._

In addition to distinguishing how text is delivered via a computer, there are some general rules to follow when using APA format to document electronic sources on a Works Cited page.

- If the information has appeared previously in print form, include print information with the other (electronic) information necessary to locate a source.
- If a URL is long and must "wrap" onto the next line, DO NOT insert any punctuation (such as a hyphen). Instead, divide the electronic address after a slash ("/") or before a period.
- APA style recommends referring to specific Web site documents rather than home or menu pages.
- URLs should not appear as hyperlinks. (Often word processing programs will automatically transform a Web address into a hyperlink. A quick way to change it back to normal type is to click on "Edit" and "Undo.")
- Occasionally, the last update is not provided on the home page. To determine the last update, enter the following in the address field and then press Enter: <javascript:alert(document.lastModified)>. The last update information will appear in a window.

**Electronic Documents Available on the Web.** The following examples are for documents that are available to anyone with a browser. Complete information is not always available on Web pages, but you should cite as much of the required information as you can reasonably obtain. (Note that citations ending in URLs do not use a final period.)

1. Web Page
Basic format:

> Author. (_last name, first initial_) (Year, month day of last update). _Title._
>
> Retrieved Month Day, Year, from URL

Notice that the URL is not followed by a period, contrary to what is customary in other APA-style entries.

Examples:

> Funk, R. S. (2001). *Health alert for reptile owners: Salmonellosis.* Retrieved
>
> December 13, 2001, from http://mesavet.com/library/
>
> salmonella.htm

> Power, T. (2002, October 30). *Salmonella in reptiles and amphibians.*
>
> Retrieved November 27, 2002, from http://www.icomm.ca/dragon/
>
> salmonella.htm

Figure 9.1 Here is an excellent example of how difficult it is to correctly classify Web documents to cite them correctly. This page is part of a larger collection entitled *Tricia's Chinese Water Dragon, Reptile and Amphibian Care Page* (backtracking through the URL—as described in chapter 8, pg. 114—reveals this). However, the information on Power's homepage reveals she is a layperson, and that the page is not part of any professional project. That means that this page should be documented as a personal Web site, authored by Tricia Power.

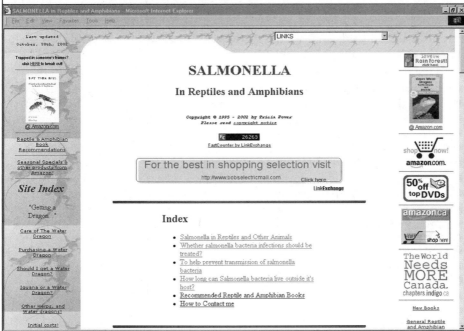

2. *A Web Page with No Author or Date*
Basic Format:

> *Document title or Name of Web page.* (n.d.). Retrieved Month Day, Year, from URL

Example:

> *Salmonella bacteria and reptiles.* (n.d.). Retrieved December 2, 2001, from
>
> http://www.hilltopanimalhospital.com/salmonella.htm

3. *Online Journal Article*
Basic format for an article that has previously appeared in a print journal or magazine and is being "reprinted" online:

> Author. (*last name, first initial*) (Year). Article title [Electronic version].
>
> *Magazine or Journal title, volume*(issue), pages. Retrieved Month Day, Year,
>
> from URL

Example:

> Levy, C., et al. (1999). Reptile-associated salmonellosis—selected states,
>
> 1996–1998 [Electronic version]. *Morbidity and Mortality Weekly Report,*
>
> *48*(44), 1009–1013. Retrieved December 12, 2001, from
>
> http://www.cdc.gov/epo/mmwrpreview/mmwrhtml/mm4844a1.htm

Basic format for an article that has never been published in print, but appears only in an online publication:

> Author. (*last name, first initial*) (Year). Article Title. *Magazine or Journal title,*
>
> *volume*(issue). Retrieved Month Day, Year, from URL

Example:

> Rosner, E. (1996). Salmonellosis from a trip to the zoo. *Physician's Weekly,*
>
> *13*(39). Retrieved December 13, 2001, from http://www.physweekly.com/
>
> archive/96/10_21_96/cu4.html

4. *Online Magazine Article*
Basic format for an article that has previously appeared in a print magazine and is being "reprinted" online:

> Author. (*last name, first initial*) (Year, month day). Article title [Electronic
>
> version]. *Magazine title,* pages. Retrieved Month Day, Year, from URL

Example:

> Turk, M. P. (2001, July). New food rules for pregnancy [Electronic version].
>
> *Parents,* 32–33. Retrieved December 13, 2001, from http://
>
> www.parents.com/articles/pregnancy/1186.jsp

Basic format for an article that has never been published in print, but appears only in an online publication:

> Author. (*last name, first initial*) (Year, month day). Article title. *Magazine Title,*
>
> Retrieved Month Day, Year, from URL

Example:

> Is your child safe from salmonella? (2000, February). *Medscape Health for*
>
> *Consumers,* Retrieved November 16, 2001, from
>
> http://cbshealthwatch.aol.com/cx/viewarticle/210245

Notice that the author's name is not available, so the title of the article appears first, followed by the date of publication.

5. Online Newspaper Article
Basic format:

> Author. (*last name, first initial*) (Year, month day). Article title. *Name of newspa-*
>
> *per.* Retrieved Month Day, Year, from URL

Example:

> Ripley, A. (2001, September 17). Salmonella and reptile pets. *The Earth Times*
>
> *News Service.* Retrieved December 12, 2001, from http://earthtimes.org/
>
> sep/healthsalmonellafromsep17_01.htm

6. Online Government Publication
Basic format:

> Sponsoring agency. (Date). *Title* (Publication No. #). Retrieved Month Day,
>
> Year, from Name of Organization via Access Mode: URL

Example:

> U.S. Food and Drug Administration, Dept. of Health and Human Services. (2001,
>
> April 1). *Chapter 1, part 1240: Control of communicable diseases* (Publication
>
> No. 21CFR1240). Retrieved September 18, 2001, from the U.S. Government
>
> Printing Office via GPO Access: http://frwebgate3.access.gpo.gov/
>
> cgi-bin/waisgate.cgi?WAISdocID=4628754938+4+0+0&WAISaction=retrieve

7. Chapter from an Online Book
Basic Format:

> Author. (*last name, first initial*) (Ed.). (*if there is an editor instead of an author*)
> (Date). Chapter title. *Book title.* Retrieved Month Day, Year,
> from URL

Example:

> King, F. W., & Burke, R. L. (Eds.). (2002, February 12). Checklist of crocodil-
> ians, tuatara, and turtles. *Crocodilian, tuatara, and turtle: An online taxo-
> nomic and geographic reference.* Retrieved November 1, 2002, from
> http://www.flmnh.ufl.edu/natsci/herpetology/turtcroclist/chklst7.htm

8. Online Forum Posting
Basic Format:

> Author. (*last name, first initial*) (Year, month day). Message subject line
> [Msg. ID] (*if available*) Message posted to group address

Example:

> East, B. (2001, May 25). Can't you get salmonella from reptiles? [Msg. 7.5]
> Message posted to http://www.landfield.com/faqs/pets/herp-faq/
> part3/section-5.html

Electronic Documents with Restricted Access. These entries usually will NOT include a URL because they require a subscription, password, or CD-ROM to access them. Cite as much of the required information as you can reasonably obtain.

1. Journal Article from a Database
Basic format:

> Author. (*last name, first initial*) (Ed.). (*if there is an editor instead of an author*)
> (Date year). Article title. *Journal Title, volume*(issue), pages. Retrieved
> Month Day, Year, from Database (Article No.) (*if given*).

Notice that the journal title and volume number are italicized.

Example:

> Lewis, C. (1997). The fright of the iguana. *FDA Consumer, 31*(7), 33–36.
> Retrieved November 18, 2001, from Academic Search Elite (Article
> No. 9711226176).

2. Magazine Article from a Database
Basic Format:

> Author. (*last name, first initial*) (Year, month day). Article title. *Magazine Title,*
>
> > pages. Retrieved Month Day, Year, from Database (Article No.) (*if given*).

Example:

> Williams, T. (1999, March). The terrible turtle trade. *Audubon,* 44+. Retrieved
>
> > October 8, 2001, from SIRSResearcher database (Article No. 098216).

3. Newspaper Article from a Database
Basic format:

> Author. (*last name, first initial*) (Year, month day). Article title. *Name of*
>
> *newspaper.* Retrieved Month Day, Year, from Database (Article No.) (*if given*).

Example:

> Webb, T. (1998, March 20). New weapon against salmonella. *Philadelphia*
>
> *Inquirer.* Retrieved September 6, 2001, from SIRSResearcher database
>
> (Article No. 021062).

4. Magazine Article from an Online Subscription Service (such as AOL)
Basic format:

> Author. (*last name, first initial*) (Year, month day). Article title. *Magazine*
>
> *Title,* page. Retrieved Month Day, Year, from Subscription Service, Keyword:
>
> search phrase.

Example:

> Hogan, D. (1997, November 14). Rage for reptiles. *Current Science,* 8.
>
> Retrieved September 19, 2001, from America Online. Keyword: reptiles
>
> AND salmonella.

Sample Research Paper Using APA Style

The following paper uses APA documentation style and provides an example of how to correctly incorporate both print and electronic documents into the text and reference list of a research paper. Annotations are provided to comment on some of the more complicated aspects of documentation.

Sheconomy.com   1

ter
rything on
page

Use a short title and page number in upper right corner of every page (use pagination feature in word processing programs to standardize this).

Sheconomy.com:

Women and E-Business Opportunities

title of essay

Midori Sato

ter's name

Economics 1101. Section 0435

Professor Johnson

October 11, 2002

Name and section number of course

Due date of assignment

ne of
ructor

Sheconomy.com:

Women and E-Business Opportunities

When the modern women's liberation movement gained

momentum in the 1960s, many American women secured greater

social freedom. However, over 40 years later most women still do

not have complete social equality with men, and this inequity is most

evident in today's economy. According to Newcomb et al. (2000),

there are only 46 women on *Forbes'* list of the "400 Richest in

America." This indicates that men continue to control American eco-

nomics, and the "glass ceiling" that has prevented women from

ascending to the top of the business ladder still exists.

Even though women aren't at the top, they are playing a sig-

nificant role in economic growth. Haynes and Haynes (2000)

report that recent government projections indicated that by the

close of the year 2000, women will own half of all U.S. small busi-

nesses (par. 6). More importantly, sales totals for women-owned

and -operated firms amounted to over $1.15 trillion in 2002

(Center for Women's Business Research [CFWBR], 2002). One

area of rapid growth for women-owned businesses is e-business.

Recently the American economy has experienced a huge shift

toward e-commerce; despite significant economic downturns, in

1999 "venture capitalists invested $1.45 billion in 107

Margin annotations:

Repeat the full title, centered, on the first page of text.

There are more than six authors, so the first author's name is given followed by "et al."

The word "and" links the names of two authors in the signal phrase.

Short title and page number in upper right corner of every page

The preferred method for APA in-text citations is to include the author's name and date in the signal phrase.

For a corporate author with a long name, spell it out the first time followed by an abbreviation in brackets or parentheses.

a direct
•tation,
icate the
hor's name,
r of
•lication, and
 specific part
he text
parated by
nmas).

en
aphrase or
nmary is
olved, you
dn't indicate
age or
agraph
nber.

s information
eared in both
rces. List
m in alpha-
cal order
arated by a
nicolon.

Washington area [Internet-related] companies" (Daniels, 2000,
par. 3). Of course, this occurred in the "technology capital" of
Washington state (home of Microsoft). Internet- and computer-
related business has been growing exponentially. And according to
Jones (2001), the percentage of venture capital directed toward
women-owned high-tech companies doubled in the year 2000.
One reason for this might be the 103 percent increase in women-
owned firms that has occurred over the past 10 years (Daniels,
2000; Haynes & Haynes, 2000). This sea change offers an
extraordinary opportunity for women to start up businesses on the
Web. The ease of start-up and some of the characteristics of e-
business offer advantages for women to make their mark in
American commerce.

First, the cost of starting business on the Web is relatively low.
This type of entrepreneur does not have to rent office space. She
just needs a computer and a phone line. E-businesses also have
lower operating costs since e-companies can provide better customer
service at a lower cost. While a live operator costs $10 per customer
contact, e-mail responses cost only $3 ("Widening," 2000).

Secondly, the nature of e-business makes it easier for
women, who frequently have added domestic responsibilities, to
manage. A survey conducted by the AFL-CIO indicates that many

Because this is
an electronic
document (no
pagination), use
"par." (for
paragraph)

In a paren-
thetical citation,
an ampersand
appears
between the last
two names of
multiple
authors.

When the
author's name
is unknown, use
a shortened
version of the
article title and
the date in the
parenthetical
phrase.

Sheconomy.com   4

This electronic document doesn't have a normal paragraph structure but is divided into three clearly marked sections.

For a quote that has been quoted in another source, identify the original speaker in the signal phrase and include "as cited in" and the name of the author of the source in the parenthetical citation.

women are employed in information technology jobs. Kristina Hanna, founder of *Girl Geeks,* notes that women in Internet-related businesses are "able to work out of their homes . . . creating their own time, their own schedules, their own world" (as cited in Solomon, 2000, sec. 3). Also, unlike most traditional businesses, an e-business does not rely on a geographical location for its success. In fact, the Internet makes a business so universally accessible that customers may be from anywhere in the United States, or even from another country. This means that it is possible to run a fairly large business from a remote location, sometimes even from home. Via the Internet, Maria del Carmen Vucetich's homemade cake business receives orders from Peruvians living all over the world (San Roman, 2000). E-commerce also offers special advantages for women since pregnancy and child rearing frequently hinders their advancement in traditional businesses. On the Web, women entrepreneurs are able to work from home while they are watching their children.

For many women, the biggest drawback to starting a business is not financial or domestic, but an issue of self-esteem. Often women think they are incapable of running their own businesses. In a survey conducted at a San Diego County high school economics class, 64 percent of the students were either running,

When using a
shortened title
to identify a
source, enclose
the title in
quotation marks.

or planning to run, an e-business. Among these students, only one

was female ("New Netpreneures," 1999). Joanna Rees Gallanter,

the founder of Venture Strategy Group, points out that "[Women]

naturally put a lower value on [success in business] than men do"

(as cited in Almer, 2000). However, there is no reason for women

to think they are less competent in business than men. Numerous

female entrepreneurs already have proven that women can be

successful in the new e-market.

For example, Olivia Ongpin, who founded *Fabric8* on the

Web in 1996, was recognized by *San Francisco Women on the*

Web as a female entrepreneur who has inspired people with her

efforts to advance technology, contribute to the community, and

set an example as a successful businesswoman on the Internet

("Top 25," n.d.). Her online shopping site contains independent

designers' clothing, music, jewelry, and accessories for women.

Another example of a woman who has been successful in e-

commerce is Ann Winbland, a software industry entrepreneur and

technology leader. She has been recognized by *Business Week* as

a member of the *Elite 25 Power Brokers in the Silicon Valley* and by

Vanity Fair as a member of the *Top 50 Leaders of the New*

Establishment (Townsend, 2001) and is one of the most powerful

women entrepreneurs in America.

e brackets to
icate words
letters that
n't appear in
e original
rding but
ve been added
clarify
aning or
nd the quote
h your
tence.

s source, a
eb site, didn't
vide an
thor or date,
a shortened
sion of the
e and the
breviation,
d." is used.

Sheconomy.com   6

This is the
second
reference to the
corporate name,
so use the
abbreviation
indicated in the
first citation.

Women entrepreneurs like Ongpin and Winbland not only
inspire other women, but also strengthen American economics.
Moreover, statistics show that women-owned businesses are,
on the average, more "financially sound and creditworthy" and
tend to remain in business longer than the average (male-owned
and -run) U.S. firm (CFWBR, 2002).

Women are the wave of the future on the Internet. As more
and more computers become networked and connected to the
Web, more and more computer users are women. In order to meet
the needs of the ever-increasing population of women on the Web,
there needs to be a growing cadre of e-businesswomen who create successful Web businesses.

Sheconomy.com   7

References

Almer, E. (2000, October 4). What women need to know about starting up. *The New York Times.* Retrieved November 15, 2002, from ProQuest database (Article No. 03624331).

Center for Women's Business Research. (2002, November 10). *Key Facts.* Retrieved November 18, 2002, from http://www.nfwbo.org/key.html

Daniels, A. (2000, November 27). The money winners: Despite troubles, Internet companies find funding in the third quarter. *Washington Techway.* Retrieved November 13, 2002, from http://www.washingtontechway.com/news/1_22/techcap/5292-1.html

Haynes, P. J. & Haynes, M. M. (2000, May). When bank loans launch new ventures: A profile of the growing female entrepreneur segment. *Bank Marketing, 32*(5), 28-35. Retrieved November 18, 2002, from WilsonSelectPlus database (Article No. BBPI00058667).

Jones, Sandra. (2001, November 12). Silicon ceiling. *Crain's Chicago Business,* 15-16. Retrieved November 16, 2002 from InfoTrac College Edition database (Article No. BBPI01089978).

Newcomb, P., Kafka, P., Egan, M. E., Murphy, V., Ridgway, N., Bravakis, P., Donovan, D., Heymsfield, C., Kimball, E., Lee, S., Maiello, M., Rand, M. (2000, October 9). By the numbers.

gin your
erence list on
eparate page
d center the
e.

en a Web
je is part
a larger
ject, the
anization's
ne appears
place of an
hor.

a work by
re than one
hor use an
persand (&)
ween the last
names.

A format
uires that
list ALL of
authors'
nes in the
erence list.

Alphabetize all entries.

This article is published only on the Web.

Always double-space everything on your References page (both within each entry and between each entry).

Sheconomy.com 8

Forbes, 361-364. Retrieved April 3, 2002, from Academic

Search Premier database (Article No. 3586171).

New netpreneures will be high schoolers. (1999, December 12).

Business Wire. Retrieved April 6, 2002, from Business

Source Premier database (Article No. CX344B1219).

San Roman, Edwin. (2000) Computers and cakes give confidence ◄─── This article
was previously
and cash to housewives in Peru. *International Trade Forum,* 3,   published in
hard copy, and
30-31. Retrieved April 3, 2002, from WilsonSelectPlus data-   is now reprinted
in a database.
base (Article No. BBPI00086539).

Solomon, Melissa. (2000, March 27). The downside of 24/7

service. *Computerworld,* 52. Retrieved April 5, 2002, from

WilsonSelectPlus database (Article No. BBPI00026264).

Top 25 Women on the Web. (n.d.). Retrieved April 3, 2002, from

Entries that   http://www.top25.org/winner.html ◄─────────────── The author and
conclude with   date for this
a URL do not   Web page are
close with   Townsend, Peg. (2001). *Ann Winblad, partner Hummer Winblad*   unknown.
a period.
        ───► *Venture Capital.* Retrieved April 3, 2002, from

http://www.techdivas.com/annwinblad.htm

Widening the road. (2000, October 2). *Electronic Design,*

48(20), 4. Retrieved April 3, 2002, from InfoTrac College

Edition database (Article No. 9711226176).

CHAPTER 10

Alternate Forms of Documentation

"Form follows function"

Louis Henri Sullivan

The most common forms of documentation are the MLA and APA styles. However, depending on the discipline for which you are writing, your instructor may require that you use other formats. The CSE (Council of Science Editors) style of documentation (formerly known as CBE—Council of Biology Editors—style) is used in many of the sciences (e.g., biology, geology, chemistry, mathematics, medicine, and physics). *The Chicago Manual of Style* (CMS) is used in history and some social science and humanities disciplines. You should always check with your instructor to make sure which style he or she requires.

Council of Science Editors Style

The CSE style of documentation is used in a wide spectrum of professional publications concerning the physical and biological sciences. As a result, the system contains a great number of variations. Some disciplines most frequently use an *author-date* format that is similar, in many ways, to the APA style of documentation.* However, the CSE format most preferred by instructors is called the *citation-sequence* system. Like other styles of documentation it uses both an in-text citation and reference list entry to indicate a source.

CSE In-Text Citations

In the CSE citation-sequence system, all bibliographic information is given in the references list at the conclusion of the paper. Within the text, the only indication that references are being cited is numbers listed sequentially throughout the

---

*This format is detailed in *Scientific Style and Format: The CBE Manual for Authors, Editors, and Publishers* (6th edition, 1994), and examples of this style can be found on the Web at <http://www.lib.ohio-state.edu/guides/cbegd.html> or <http://writing.colostate.edu/references/sources/cbe/index.cfm>.

text.* These numbers correspond to the numbered entries in the references list. This method interrupts the flow of the text the least; however, there are some drawbacks. Readers receive almost no information about a source unless they turn to the list at the end of the essay. Also, because authors' names are not mentioned in the text, they receive less recognition than they would if another system of documentation were used. The reference list is organized numerically, starting with the first reference cited in the text.

Examples of CSE Citation-Sequence In-Text Citations

Some basic rules for in-text citation in the CSE citation-sequence system follow.

- Use a superscript number or a number in parentheses [e.g., (1)] following any reference to a source. Superscript numbers are recommended because parenthetical numbers can be confused with other parenthetical statements in your essay.

e- TIPS

Typing Superscript Numbers
To create a superscript number using Microsoft Word, simply type the number into the text as you would normally do (leave **no** space between end punctuation or the end of a word and the number), then highlight the number, click on "Format" on the main menu, click on "Font" and then check the box next to the term "superscript" in the list of options and click "OK."

Examples:

- Reptiles captured in the wild and transported for sale as pets run a higher risk of bacterial infection.[1]

- Reptiles captured in the wild and transported for sale as pets run a higher risk of bacterial infection (1).

Note that when using a superscript number, the end punctuation precedes the number. When using a number in parentheses, the end punctuation follows the parentheses. If you cite the same source later in an essay, refer to it by its original number.

---

*Another option is to use the name-year system, which lists the author's surname and year of publication in parentheses after the citation [e.g., (Bradley 2001)]. In this system, the references list is organized alphabetically. See *Scientific Style and Format: The CBE Manual for Authors, Editors, and Publishers* (6th edition, 1994) for guidelines.

Example:

> Reptiles captured in the wild and transported for sale as pets run a higher risk of bacterial infection.[1] This is because they are frequently kept in unsanitary containers or cages and fed infrequently and/or incorrectly.[2] Studies[1] show that good hygiene and a healthy diet will reduce the incidence of bacterial infections in reptiles.

The in-text reference number should immediately follow the title, word, or phrase that indicates the information or document you are citing.

- If a single reference indicates more than one source, list the source numbers in a series.

Examples:

- As the public has become more conscious of the biological risks posed by pet reptiles, the number of salmonella infections has decreased. [1,4,7]

- Experts agree that reducing the incidence of bacterial infection in the domestic reptile population requires the cooperation of pet dealers.[2-4]

Use a comma (but no intervening spaces) to separate two numbers, or numbers that do not form a sequence. Use a dash to separate more than two numbers that form a sequence.

- If you are citing from a source that has been quoted in a subsequent document, record the reference number for the original document followed by the parenthetical statement "cited in" and the reference number for the secondary document.

Example:

- The first report of human salmonella infection linked to pet turtles[5(cited in 6)] occurred in Chicago.

Do not space between the first reference number and the parenthetical citation. The complete bibliographic information for BOTH sources must appear in your references list.

CSE Reference List Entries

At the conclusion of a research paper, you need to furnish a list that includes all of the references used. Should your instructor require that you list sources you read but did not cite, include these entries in a separate list entitled "Additional References."

Every entry on a reference list provides the same basic information—author (last name, first), year of publication, title, and publication information. However, the format differs depending on the type of source you are listing. Most instructors place a high premium on correctly formatting a reference list, so pay special attention to detail and produce a page that will boost, rather than reduce, your grade.

The following are a few *general rules* to follow in order to properly format your reference list.

- Begin a new page for your reference list after the last page of your essay.
- Place the title (References or Cited References) flush with the left margin and distinguish it by using a bold font, underlining, or all capital letters.
- Double-space *everything* on the page (between the title and the first entry, within each entry, and between entries).
- Place the reference number flush with the left margin, skip two spaces, and begin the entry.
- Authors' (or editors') names should always appear last name first. Indicate first and middle initials (if given), and do not punctuate between them (i.e., there should be no comma between last name and initials, no periods after initials and no space between initials). All authors' or editors' names should appear in the entry.
- If the name of the author or editor of a work is not provided, then list the author as "[Anonymous]".
- The titles of books or articles should appear in sentence-style capitalization: capitalize only the first word and all proper nouns (ex. Reptile care: an atlas of diseases and treatments) and do NOT underline, italicize, or enclose in quotation marks.

⏱ *Quick* CHECK

CSE Guidelines for Abbreviating Journal Titles
Journal titles longer than one word need to be abbreviated. Single-syllable words and words of five or fewer letters are generally not abbreviated. Retain all significant elements of the title, but remove
- Articles, conjunctions, and prepositions (unless they are part of a proper noun, a standard phrase, or a scientific or technical term; ex. the "in" from "in vitro")
- At least the final two letters, if possible: ex. Biological becomes Biol
- Internal letters: ex. Country becomes Ctry
Capitalize the initial letter of each abbreviated word and omit all punctuation (don't put periods at the ends of abbreviations).

- The titles of journals that consist of more than one word should be abbreviated (see the Quick Check Box for guidelines on abbreviating titles).
- Within the reference entry, skip one space after each period, comma, and colon.
- End every entry with a period.

Printed Sources. In order to correctly format your reference list, it is important to identify the type of source that you are documenting. Standard CSE format for print sources (as opposed to electronic documents) has remained virtually unchanged for years and is readily available in numerous print and online sources. You may have a guide to basic CSE format in your textbook or access to *Scientific Style and Format: The CBE Manual for Authors, Editors, and Publishers* (6th edition, 1994) in your library. In addition there are numerous Web sites to help you determine the proper format for your sources. The following are two of the best.

CSU: Council of Biology Editors (CBE) Scientific Style

<http://writing.colostate.edu/references/sources/cbe/index.cfm>

The Council of Biology Editors (CBE) Style of Documentation in Science and Mathematics: Monroe Community College

<http://www.monroecc.edu/depts/library/cbe.htm>

Books:
Obtain all information from the title page (and the reverse side of the title page), not from the cover.

1. Book with One Author
Basic format:

> #. Last name and initial(s) of author. Title. Edition. (*if given*) Place of publi-
> cation: Publisher; Year of publication. Number of pages in the book.

Always list the city of publication; if the city is unfamiliar (or if it is the name of a city in more than one state), list the state as well. Use the two-letter ZIP code abbreviation in parentheses, but do not use a comma to separate the city from the state abbreviation.

Example:

> 1. Cloudsley-Thompson JL. The diversity of amphibians and reptiles: an
> introduction. New York: Springer; 1999. 254 p.

2. Book with One Editor
Basic format:

> #. Last name and initial(s) of editor, editor. Title. Edition. (*if given*) Place of
> publication: Publisher; Year of publication. Number of pages in the book.

Example:

> 2. Fudge AM, editor. Laboratory medicine: avian and exotic pets.
> Philadelphia: Saunders; 2000. 486 p.

3. A Book with Two or More Authors or Editors
Basic format:

> #.   Last name and initial(s) of authors (*separated by commas*). editors. (*if editors, not authors*) Title. Edition. (*if given*) Place of publication: Publisher; Year of publication. Number of pages in the book.

Examples:

> 3.   Zug GR, Vitt LJ, Caldwell JP. Herpetology: an introductory biology of amphibians and reptiles. 2nd ed. San Diego: Academic Press; 2001. 630 p.

> 4.   Wright KM, Whitaker BR, editors. Amphibian medicine and captive husbandry. Malabar (FL): Krieger; 2001. 499 p.

4. A Chapter or Article in a Larger Work
Basic format:

> #.   Last name and initial(s) of author(s) of chapter or article. Title of chapter or article. In: Last name and initial(s) of authors or editor(s) of book, editors. (*if editor, not author*) Volume, (*if given*) Title of book. Edition. (*if given*) Place of publication: Publisher; Year of publication. Page numbers of the chapter or article.

Example:

> 5.   Collins F, Jordan E. Human genome project. In: Volume 7, McGraw-Hill encyclopedia of science and technology. 9th ed. New York: McGraw-Hill; 2002. p 229–32.

Periodicals:
For journal titles longer than one word, abbreviate the title according to CSE guidelines (see the Quick Check on page 154.).

5. Journal Article (with continuous pagination)
Basic format:

> #.   Last name and initial(s) of author(s). Title of article. Title of journal Year of publication;volume #: Page numbers.

Example:

> 6.   Bradley T, Angulo F, Mitchell M. Public health education on salmonella spp and reptiles. J Am Vet Med Assoc 2001;219:754–5.

Abbreviate page ranges (ex. 233–45; 76-9); if an article appears on noncontiguous pages, list all pages or page ranges (ex. 23–7, 44, 46–9).

6. *Journal Article (where each issue begins with page 1)*
Basic format:

> #. Last name and initial(s) of author(s). Title of article. Title of Journal Year and month of publication;volume #(issue #):Page numbers.

Example:

> 7. Herbst LH, Klein PA. Green turtle fibropapillomatosis: challenges to assessing the role of environmental cofactors. Envir Health Persp Sup 1995 Dec;103(4):27–30.

7. *Magazine Article*
Basic format:

> #. Last name and initial(s) of author(s). Title of article. Title of magazine Year Month Day of publication:Page numbers.

Example:

> 8. Williams T. The terrible turtle trade. Audubon 1999 Mar-Apr:44, 59.

> 9. [Anonymous]. Salmonella in pet reptiles—still a problem. Child Health Alert 2000 Jan:4–5.

For a magazine published monthly or every two months, indicate the year and month. Use a three-letter abbreviation for each month, but do not conclude with a period. For a magazine published weekly, indicate the year, month, and day. If a magazine lists volume and issue numbers, these may be used in lieu of the month and day following the same format as journal articles in example 6.

> 10. Padgett T, Liston B. Tickled about turtles. Time 2000 Feb 28:76.

> **OR**

> 11. Padgett T, Liston B. Tickled about turtles. Time 2000 Feb;155(8):76.

8. *Newspaper Article*
Basic format:

> #. Last name and initial(s) of author(s). Title of article. Title of newspaper Year Month Day of publication; Section information: Page number (column number).

Example:

> 12. Aeppel T. Seeking ways to rid turtles of salmonella. Wall Street Journal 1996 May 30; Sect B:3(col 1).
>
> 13. Tunstall J. Saving turtles is slow work. Tampa Tribune 2002 Oct 7; Metro:2 (col 4).
>
> 14. Harden B. They brake for turtles in Padre Island Park. New York Times 2002 Dec 1; Sect 1:37(col 5).

Electronic Sources. One challenge confronting the research paper writer in the age of the Internet is that the essential components of a references list entry (author's name, title, date of publication) may be missing from electronic documents or may be present in a form that must be converted into something that makes sense in the CSE formatting system (e.g., a URL and the date when a site was last updated might have to replace more standard publication information). Last, but not least, information that has been "reprinted" on the Web might lack complete documentation about the original source. (See the E-Tip on pg. 114 on finding citation information.)

Yet another obstacle to correctly formatting a references list is identifying the type of source being used. Remember that the dual purpose of documentation is to give credit to the author *and* to enable a reader to find the material cited. Therefore, you need to determine first whether the source is available via the Web (so it has a URL that can be accessed by anyone with a browser), or if it is delivered via a computer but available only through a licensing agreement or password (such as a subscription database, subscription service like AOL, or a CD-ROM). Reference list entries in the former category will include a URL, whereas those in the latter group will not.

However, the greatest obstacle to correctly formatting electronic documents in the CSE style is that little guidance has been provided. Because the CSE style manual hasn't been updated since 1994, many of the types of documents now available via the Internet are not included.* The manual covers electronic sources such as electronic journals and books (delivered either via the Internet or CD-ROM), but it does not include examples of Web pages or databases. The examples that follow are based on the *National Library of Medicine Recommended Formats for Bibliographic Citation* for Internet sources—a format to which the updated CSE manual should closely adhere.** In addition to distinguishing how a text is delivered via a computer, there are some general rules to follow when using CSE format to document electronic sources on a references list.

---

*A seventh edition of *Scientific Style and Format* is due out soon; information and updates are available at the official CSE Web site <http://www.councilscienceeditors.org/publications/citing_internet.cfm>

**A complete guide to documentation of Internet sources according to *NLM* format is available at <http://www.nlm.nih.gov/pubs/formats/internet.pdf>

- Because there are no regulations concerning publication on the Web, many sites do not clearly state the author's name. Do not assume that the Webmaster or contact person is the author (or even the editor). Many sites are maintained by organizations that should be considered the publishers, not the authors, of the sites. The *NLM* does not recommend the use of "[Anonymous]" in citations when you cannot locate the author of a Web page.

- If the information has appeared previously in print form, include print information with the other (electronic) information necessary to locate a source.

- If a URL is long and must "wrap" onto the next line, DO NOT insert any punctuation (such as a hyphen). Instead, divide the electronic address in a logical place, such as at a slash ("/"), period, or hyphen.

- URL and e-mail addresses should not appear as hyperlinks. (Often, word processing programs will automatically transform a Web address into a hyperlink. A quick way to change it back to normal type is to click on "Edit" and "undo".) (See E-Tip on pg. 115 concerning accurate URLs.)

- Occasionally, the last update is not provided on the home page. To determine the last update, enter <javascript:alert(document.lastModified)> [without the angle brackets] in the address field and then press Enter. The last update information will appear in a window.

- If a URL is the final element, the entry does not conclude with a period unless the URL ends with a slash.

Electronic Documents Available on the Web. The following examples are for documents that are available to anyone with a browser. Complete information is not always available on Web pages, but you should cite as much of the required information as you can reasonably obtain.

9. Single Web Page
A single Web page is complete in itself and is not connected to a larger, professional Web project.

Basic format:

> #. Last name and initial(s) of author(s). Title of site (*Use a descriptor such as Home page—neither underlined nor in quotation marks—if there is no title*) [Internet]. [updated year month day; cited year month day]. Available from: URL

Examples:

> 15. Kaplan M. Cryptosporidium: health threat to humans and reptiles [Internet]. [updated 2002 Aug 17; cited 2002 Oct 24]. Available from: http://www.anapsid.org/cryptosporidium.html

16. Fife R. Salmonella and your privilege to keep reptiles to be reviewed by the FDA [Internet]. [updated 2003 Mar 3; cited 2003 Jul 7]. Available from: http://personal.riverusers.com/~richardfife/page20.html

17. Power T. Salmonella in reptiles and amphibians [Internet]. [updated 2001 Feb 19; cited 2001 Dec 12]. Available from: http://www.icomm.ca/dragon/salmonella.htm

---

Figure 10.1 Here is an excellent example of how difficult it is to correctly classify Web documents to cite them correctly. This page is part of a larger collection entitled *Melissa Kaplan's Herp Care Collection* (backtracking through the URL—as described in Box 8.3—reveals this). However, the information on Kaplan's home page reveals she is a layperson and that the page is not part of any professional project. That means that this page should be documented as a personal Web site, authored by Melissa Kaplan.

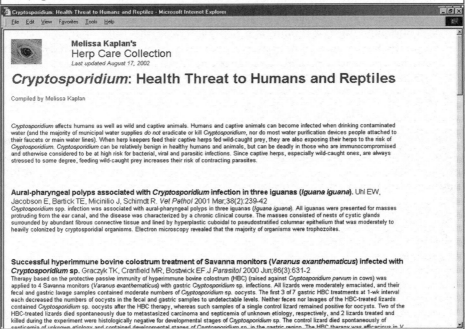

---

10. Secondary Web Page

A secondary Web page is part of a larger, professional Web project. The page has a title but also features the name of the project, as well.

Basic format:

#.   Last name and initial(s) of author(s). Title of page. Title of Web project. [Internet]. Name of any organization or institution associated with the site; [updated year month day; cited year month day]. Available from: URL

Examples:

18. Kuhrt T. Trachemys scripta. Animal diversity web. [Internet]. University of Michigan Museum of Zoology; [updated 2001 May 2; cited 2001 Dec 2]. Available from: http://animaldiversity.ummz.umich.edu/accounts/trachemys/t._scripta$narrative.html

19. Salmonella infection (salmonellosis) and animals. National Center for Infectious Diseases. [Internet]. Centers for Disease Control and Prevention; [updated 2002 Oct 7; cited 2002 Oct 24]. Available from: http://www.cdc.gov/healthypets/diseases/salmonellosis.htm

Figure 10.2 This Web site page is one page in a larger project (*The Animal Diversity Web*) that is sponsored by the University of Michigan (the electronic "publisher") of the site.

11. Online Journal Article

An online journal article is the electronic text of a previously printed article (now available on the Web) or a document available only on the Internet.

Basic format:

> #. Last name and initial(s) of author(s). Title of article. Title of journal [Internet]. Year of publication [cited year month day];vol. #(issue): (*if each issue begins at page 1*)page numbers. Available from: URL

Examples:

> 20. Levy C, Finnerty M, Hansen G, Cory J, McGuill M, Matyas B, DeMaria A, Schmunk G, Grantham J, Archer J, Kazmierczak J, Davis J. Reptile-associated salmonellosis—selected states, 1996–1998. Morb and Mort Wkly Rpt [Internet]. 1999 [cited 2001 Dec 12];48:1009–13. Available from: http://www.cdc.gov/epo/mmwrpreview/mmwrhtml/ mm4844a1.htm

> 21. Rosner E. Salmonellosis from a trip to the zoo. Phys Wkly [Internet]. 1996 [cited 2001 Dec 13]; 13(39). Available from: http://www.physweekly.com/archive/96/10_21_96/cu4.html

For articles that have been previously published, include page numbers. Because electronic documents do not have pagination, you will not indicate page numbers.

12. Online Magazine Article

An online magazine article is the electronic text of a previously printed article (now available on the Web) or a document available only on the Internet.

Basic format:

> #. Last name and initial(s) of author(s). Title of article. Title of magazine [Internet]. Year of publication [cited year month day]:Page numbers. Available from: URL

Examples:

> 22. Turk MP. New food rules for pregnancy. Parents. [Internet]. 2001 [cited 2001 Dec 13]:32-3. Available from: http://www.parents.com/articles/ pregnancy/1186.jsp

> 23. Williams W. Turtle tragedy: demand in Asia may be wiping out turtle populations worldwide. Scientific American.com. [Internet]. 1999 [cited 2002 Oct 21]; Available from: http://www.sciam.com/ article.cfm?articleID=00043E38-66A6-1C72-9EB7809EC588F2D7& pageNumber=2&catID=2

13. *Online Newspaper Article*

An online newspaper article is the electronic text of a previously printed article (now available on the Web) or a document available only on the Internet.

Basic format:

> #. Last name and initial(s) of author(s). Title of article. Title of newspaper
>
> [Internet]. Year month day of publication [cited year month day]:
>
> [Number of paragraphs]. Available from: URL

Examples:

> 24. Hoy C. Sea turtles use a natural compass to find their way. USA Today
>
> [Internet]. 2001 Oct 12 [cited 2002 Dec 18]: [8 paragraphs].
>
> Available from: http://www.usatoday.com/news/science/aaas/
>
> 2001-10-11-turtles.htm

> 25. Lelis L. Turtles arrive in state—with help. Sun Sentinel [Internet].
>
> 2002 Dec 20 [cited 2002 Dec 22]: [10 paragraphs]. Available from:
>
> http://www.sun-sentinel.com/news/local/florida/
>
> orlloccoldturtle20122002dec20.story

14. *Online Encyclopedia Entry*

Basic format:

> #. Last name and initial(s) of author(s). (*if given*) Title of entry. Title of
>
> online reference [Internet]. City of publication: Publisher; Year of
>
> publication. [cited year month day]. Available from: URL

Example:

> 26. Salmonellosis. Encyclopedia Britannica [Internet]. Encyclopedia
>
> Britannica Premium Service. [cited 2003 Jul 10]. Available from:
>
> http://www.britannica.com/eb/article?eu=66794

15. *Online Government Publication*

An online government publication is the electronic text of a previously printed article (now available on the Web) or a document available only on the Internet.

Basic format:

> #. Name of the government. Name of the government agency. [Internet].
>
> City of publication: Publisher; Year of publication. [cited year month
>
> day]. Title of publication. Available from: URL

Example:

> 27. Utah. Department of Health. [Internet]. Salt Lake City: Bureau of
> Epidemiology, 2001. [cited 2001 Dec 8]. Reptile-associated salmonel-
> losis. Available from: http://hlunix.hl.state.ut.us/els/epidemiology/
> epifacts/reptile.html

16. Online Book

An online book may be the electronic text of part or all of a printed book (now available on the Web) or a book-length document available only on the Internet.
Basic format:

> #. Last name and initial(s) of author(s) editor(s). (*if editor, not author*)
> Chapter title (*if given*). In: Title of book [Internet]. Edition. (*if given*)
> Place of publication: Publisher; Year of publication [updated year month
> day; cited year month day]. Page numbers. Available from: URL

Examples:

> 28. Ernst CH, Zug GR. Should I keep a snake (or any other reptile) as a
> pet? In: Snakes in question: the Smithsonian answer book [Internet].
> Washington: Smithsonian Institute Press; 1996 [updated 2001 Dec 22;
> cited 2002 Oct 13]. p. 149–51. Available from: http://www.embl-
> heidelberg.de/~uetz/db-info/snakes_as_pets.html

> 29. Drugge R. The electronic textbook of dermatology [Internet].
> Internet Dermatological Society; 2000 [updated 2002 Jul 6; cited
> 2002 Oct 24]. Available from: http://www.telemedicine.org/
> stamford.htm

17. Online Forum Posting

Basic format:

> #. Last name and initial(s) of author. Title of posting. In: Name of forum
> [Internet]; Year month day, time of posting [cited year month day].
> Available from: URL

Example:

> 30. Peteralbrian. Treating parasites without fecals. In: Herpetological
> Health Forum [Internet]; 2003 Apr 23, 16:49:31 [cited 2003 Jul 7].
> Available from: http://forum.kingsnake.com/health/
> messages/5960.html

Electronic Documents with Restricted Access. These entries usually do not include a URL because they require a subscription, password, or CD-ROM to access them. Cite as much of the required information as you can reasonably obtain.

18. Journal Article from a Database
Basic format:

> #. Last name and initial(s) of author(s). Title of article. Title of journal Year and month of publication;vol. #(issue #): (*if each issue begins at page 1*) page numbers. In: Name of database [database]. [modified year month day; cited year month day]. Available from: Name of service. Name of library. or URL of provider

Example:

> 31. Herbst LH, Klein PA. Green turtle fibropapillomatosis: challenges to assessing the role of environmental cofactors. Envir Health Prsp Sup 1995 Dec;103(4):27–30. In: Academic Search Premier [database] [cited 2002 Oct 27]. Available from: EBSCOhost. Seminole Community College Library.

19. Magazine Article from a Database
Basic format:

> #. Last name and initial(s) of author(s). Title of article. Title of magazine Year Month Day (*if weekly*) of publication:Page numbers. In: Name of database [database]. [cited year month day]. Available from: Name of service. Name of library. or URL of provider

Example:

> 32. Williams W. The deadly shell game. Animals 1999 May:16. In: InfoTrac College Edition [database]. [cited 2002 Nov 15]. Available from Gale Group. http://www.infotrac-college.com

20. Newspaper Article from a Database
Basic format:

> #. Last name and initial(s) of author(s). Title of article. Title of newspaper Year Month Day of publication; Section information: Page numbers. In: Name of Database [database]. [cited year month day]. Available from: Name of service. Name of library. or URL of provider

Example:

> 33. Webb T. New weapon against salmonella. Philadelphia Inquirer 1998
>
> Mar 20:n.p. In: SIRSResearcher [database]. [cited 2001 Dec 13].
>
> Available from: FirstSearch. Seminole Community College Library.

If page numbers aren't provided, use "n.p." to indicate the information is
unavailable.

21. *Magazine Article from an Online Subscription Service (such as AOL)*
Basic format:

> #. Last name and initial(s) of author(s). Title of article. Title of magazine
>
> Year month day *(if weekly)* of publication:Page numbers. In: Name of
>
> Subscription Service [Online Service]. [cited year month day]. Keyword:
>
> search phrase.

Example:

> 34. Hogan D. Rage for reptiles. Current Science 1997 Nov 14:8. In: AOL
>
> [Online Service]. [cited 2001 Dec 15]. Keyword: reptiles AND
>
> salmonella.

22. *Encyclopedia Article from a CD-ROM*
Basic format:

> #. Last name and initial(s) of author(s) of article. *(if given)* Title of entry.
>
> Title of encyclopedia. Edition or version. [CD-ROM]. Name of vendor;
>
> Year of electronic publication. [cited year month day].

Example:

> 35. Salmonella. Compton's Interactive Encyclopedia. Ver 2000Dlx. [CD-
>
> ROM]. Compton's NewMedia; 2000. [cited 2001 Dec 12].

23. *E-Mail Message*
Basic format:

> #. Last name and initial(s) of sender. Subject of message [electronic mail on
>
> the Internet]. Message to: Name of recipient. Year month day, time of
>
> transmission [cited year month day].

Example:

> 36. Peppers J. Salmonellosis in turtles [electronic mail on the Internet].
>
> Message to Frank Bonner. 2000 May 10, 11:30 am [cited 2002 Jun 30].

Chicago Manual of Style

The CMS form of documentation was once widely used in many social science and humanities disciplines. Today it is employed to a much more limited extent. However, some professors continue to require that you document according to this system. The CMS format uses a combination of footnotes or endnotes and a bibliography that appears at the end of the essay.

CMS Footnotes or Endnotes

In CMS format, complete bibliographic information is given in the text of the paper (either at the bottom of the page on which the reference appears—in a footnote—or at the end of the essay—in the endnotes) as well as on the bibliography page at the conclusion of the essay. Within the text, a superscript numeral is used to indicate that a quotation, paraphrase, or summary is being employed. That numeral corresponds to a footnote or endnote (you must choose one method and use it consistently throughout the essay) that provides complete publication information.

- Footnotes should be provided at the bottom of the page on which the citation appears.

- Endnotes should be provided on their own page, immediately following the last page of the essay. Begin a new page for your endnotes after the essay, and center your title ("Endnotes") one inch from the top of the page.

Some Basic Rules for Footnotes and Endnotes in the CMS

- Use a superscript number following any reference to a source. (See the E-Tip on page 152.)
  - Notes are numbered consecutively as they appear in the text.
  - End punctuation precedes the note number.

Example: Reptiles captured in the wild and transported for sale as pets run a higher risk of bacterial infection.[1] This is because they are frequently kept in unsanitary containers or cages and fed infrequently and/or incorrectly.[2]

- The number in the text corresponds to a footnote or endnote.
  — Single-space within notes and double-space between them.
  — For each note, type the number on the line, followed by a period and one space.

Basic format:

> 1. Author, (*first name, first*) ed., (*if there is an editor instead of an author*). *Title,* volume and/or edition number (*if there is one*) (Place of publication: Publisher, date of publication), page #.

Example:

> 1. Harmut Wilket, *Turtles: Everything about Purchase, Care, Nutrition, and Diseases* (Woodbury, NY: Barron's, 1983), 83.
>
> 2. Douglas R. Mader, ed., *Reptile Medicine and Surgery* (Philadelphia: W. B. Saunders, 1996), 36.

- CMS style discourages using more than one note at a single text location (i.e., "These risks can be reduced.[3,4]"). Instead, combine the material to create one single note. If the subject matter changes within the new note, indicate this by starting a new paragraph at the change.
- If you are citing from a source that has been quoted in a subsequent document, record one reference number. In your note, include both works, using "quoted in."

Example:

The first report of human salmonella infection linked to pet turtles[5] occurred in Chicago.

> 5. Tad Hardy, "The Tortoise and the Scare," *Bio Science* 38, no. 2 (1988):76–9, quoted in Ted Williams, "The Terrible Turtle Trade," *Audubon,* March/April (1999):44.

The complete bibliographic information for BOTH sources must appear in your bibliography.

- For subsequent references to a source you have already cited, give only the author's name and the pages cited. If you cite more than one work by the same author, subsequent citations should include a shortened form of the title (italicized if it is a book title, in quotation marks if it is the title of an article.)

Example:

> 3. Mader, 32.

4. Williams, "Terrible Turtle," 8.

5. Williams, *Lake and Pond,* 43.

CMS Footnote/Endnote and Bibliography Format

The format for footnote/endnote entries and bibliography entries is very similar. In fact, at first glance they seem almost identical. Because they are so alike, the two formats (note entry and bibliography entry) are best understood when seen together. Therefore, in the following examples of CMS formatting, the model note entry appears first, followed by the model bibliography entry.

Some Basic Rules for Bibliography Pages in the CMS Style

- Begin a new page for your bibliography (after the essay if using footnotes or after the endnotes page(s) if using endnotes). Center your title ("Bibliography") one inch from the top of the page.
- Single-space each entry and double-space between entries.
- Alphabetize the entries according to authors' last names.
- If no author's name is given, alphabetize according to the first significant word in the title (ignore *A, An,* and *The*).
- Should you reference more than one work by the same author, arrange the works alphabetically (by title) or chronologically (by date of publication). (Either method is acceptable, but be consistent throughout the bibliography.) The first entry should follow the prescribed format, but in subsequent works, use three dashes followed by a period instead of the author's name.
- Note that CMS **prefers to italicize rather than underline.**

Printed Sources. As with every other form of documentation, it is important to identify the type of source that you are documenting. Standard CMS format for print sources (as opposed to electronic documents) has remained virtually unchanged for years and is readily available in numerous print and online sources. There are numerous Web sites to help you determine the proper format for your sources. The following are two of the best.

UW-Madison: Writer's Handbook Documentation
<http://www.wisc.edu/writing/Handbook/DocChicago.html>

FSU Library: Chicago Manual of Style Documentation
<http://www.fsu.edu/library/search/toolkits/chicago.shtml>

Books:
Obtain all information from the title page (and the reverse side of the title page), not from the cover.

1. Book with One Author or Editor
Endnote/Footnote:

> 1. Frederic L. Frye, *Biomedical and Surgical Aspects of Captive Reptile Husbandry,* 2nd ed. (Malabar, FL: Krieger Pub., 1991), 26.

> 2. Alan F. Fudge, ed., *Laboratory Medicine: Avian and Exotic Pets* (Philadelphia: Saunders, 2000), 143.

Bibliography:

> Frye, Frederic L. *Biomedical and Surgical Aspects of Captive Reptile Husbandry.* 2nd ed. Malabar, FL: Krieger Pub., 1991.

> Fudge, Alan F., ed. *Laboratory Medicine: Avian and Exotic Pets.* Philadelphia: Saunders, 2000.

2. A Book with Two or Three Authors or Editors
Endnote/Footnote:

> 3. C. Wray and A. Wray, *Salmonella in Domestic Animals* (New York: CABI Publications, 2000), 52.

> 4. Clifford Warwick, Fredric L. Frye, and James B. Murphy, eds., *Health and Welfare of Captive Reptiles* (New York: Chapman & Hall, 1995), 137.

Bibliography:

> Wray, C., and A. Wray. *Salmonella in Domestic Animals.* New York: CABI Publications, 2000.

> Warwick, Clifford, Fredric L. Frye, and James B. Murphy, eds. *Health and Welfare of Captive Reptiles.* New York: Chapman & Hall, 1995.

3. A Book by More Than Three Authors or Editors
Endnote/Footnote:

> 5. Karl Garbrisch et al., eds. *Atlas of Diagnostic Radiology of Exotic Pets: Small Mammals, Birds, Reptiles and Amphibians* (London: Wolfe Pub., 1991), 39.

Bibliography:

> Garbrisch, Karl, G. Alexander Rübel, Ewald Isenbügel, and Pim Wolvekamp, eds. *Atlas of Diagnostic Radiology of Exotic Pets: Small Mammals, Birds, Reptiles and Amphibians.* London: Wolfe Pub., 1991.

4. A Work in an Anthology
Endnote/Footnote:

> 6. Kay Ryan, "Turtle," in *Literature: An Introduction to Fiction, Poetry, and Drama* 8th ed., ed. X. J. Kennedy and Dana Gioia (New York: Longman, 2002), 874.

Bibliography:

> Ryan, Kay. "Turtle." In *Literature: An Introduction to Fiction, Poetry, and Drama,* 8th ed. Edited by X. J. Kennedy and Dana Gioia. New York: Longman, 2002.

5. An Entry in an Encyclopedia or Dictionary
Endnote/Footnote:

> 7. *The New Encyclopedia Britannica,* 15th ed., s.v. "turtle."

The abbreviation *s.v.* is for the Latin *sub verbo* (under the word).
Bibliography:
According to CMS, encyclopedias and dictionaries are not included in bibliographies.

Periodicals:

6. Journal Article

(A journal with continuous pagination)
Endnote/Footnote:

> 8. Shannon K. Meehan, "Swelling Popularity of Reptiles Leads to Increase in Reptile-Associated Salmonellosis," *Journal of the American Veterinary Medical Association* 209 (1996): 531.

Bibliography:

> Meehan, Shannon K. "Swelling Popularity of Reptiles Leads to Increase in Reptile-Associated Salmonellosis." *Journal of the American Veterinary Medical Association* 209 (1996): 531–41.

(A journal in which each issue begins with page 1)
Endnote/Footnote:

> 9. Tad Hardy, "The Tortoise and the Scare," *BioScience* 38, no. 2 (1988): 78.

Bibliography:

> Hardy, Tad. "The Tortoise and the Scare." *BioScience* 38, no. 2 (1988): 76–9.

7. *Magazine Article*
Endnote/Footnote:

> 10. Peter Pritchard, "Tickled about Turtles," *Time,* 28 February 2000, 77.

> 11. Ted Williams, "The Terrible Turtle Trade," *Audubon,* March/April
> 1999, 44.

If the page numbers of an article are not sequential, do not indicate page numbers in the bibliography.

Bibliography:

> Pritchard, Peter. "Tickled about Turtles." *Time,* 28 February 2000, 76–8.

> Williams, Ted. "The Terrible Turtle Trade. " *Audubon,* March/April 1999.

If the page numbers of an article are not sequential, do not indicate page numbers.

8. *Newspaper Article*
Endnote/Footnote:

> 12. Timothy Aeppel, "Seeking Ways to Rid Turtles of Salmonella," *Wall Street
> Journal,* 30 May 1996, sec. B.

Page numbers are usually omitted from notes related to newspaper articles.

Bibliography:

News items from daily newspapers are usually not listed in the bibliography.

Electronic Sources. The Internet has made it possible to transmit information in new ways, and these methods and modes are in a constant state of flux. The challenge confronting the research paper writer in the age of the World Wide Web is that the essential components of a documentation entries (author's name, title, publication information) may be missing from electronic documents, or they might be present in a form that must be converted into something that makes sense in the CMS formatting system. For example, a Web site may not indicate an author (or the author might use an alias). The layout of an online document might make it difficult to distinguish between two or three possible titles, or there might be no title. A URL and the date when a site was last updated might have to replace more standard publication information. Last, but not least, information that has been "reprinted" on the Web might lack complete documentation about the original source. (See the E-Tip on p. 114 about finding citation information.)

Yet another obstacle to correctly formatting a references list is identifying the type of source being used. Remember that the dual purpose of documentation is to give credit to the author *and* to enable a reader to find the material cited. Therefore, you need to determine first whether the source is available via the Web (so it has a URL that can be accessed by anyone with a browser), or if it is delivered via a computer but available only through a licensing agreement or password (such as a subscription database, subscription service like AOL, or a CD-ROM). References list entries in the former category will include a URL, whereas those in the latter group will not.

However, the greatest obstacle to correctly formatting electronic documents in the CMS style is that little guidance has been provided. Because the CMS style manual hasn't been updated since 1993, many of the types of documents now available via the Internet are not included. The examples that follow are based on a system developed by Andrew Harnack and Eugene Kleppinger in *Online! A Reference Guide to Using Internet Sources,* a system recommended on the official CMS Web site.

In addition to distinguishing how a text is delivered via a computer, there are some general rules to follow when using CMS format to document electronic sources.

- If the information has appeared previously in print form, include print information with the other (electronic) information necessary to locate a source.
- If a URL is long and must "wrap" onto the next line, DO NOT insert any punctuation (such as a hyphen). Instead, divide the electronic address in a logical place, such as at a slash ("/"), period, or hyphen.
- Enclose URLs and e-mail addresses in angle brackets .
- URL and e-mail addresses should not appear as hyperlinks. (Often word processing programs will automatically transform a Web address into a hyperlink. A quick way to change it back to normal type is to click on "Edit" and "undo".)
- The final element in all electronic document entries is the date of access, enclosed in parentheses.

Electronic Documents Available on the Web. The following examples are for documents that are available to anyone with a browser. Complete information is not always available on Web pages, but you should cite as much of the required information as you can reasonably obtain.

◑ *Quick* CHECK

CMS Web Page Basic Format
Web page entries should include the following information.
- Author's or editor's name
- Title of document, in quotation marks
- Title of larger Web project (if relevant), in italics
- Date of publication or last revision
- URL, in angle brackets
- Date of access, in parentheses

1. Single Web Page

A single Web page is complete in itself and is not connected to a larger, professional Web project.

Endnote/Footnote:

> 13. Tricia Power, "Salmonella in Reptiles and Amphibians," 30 October 2002,
>
> <http://www.icomm.ca/dragon/salmonella.htm> (14 November 2002).

Bibliography:

> Power, Tricia. "Salmonella in Reptiles and Amphibians." 30 October 2002.
>
> <http://www.icomm.ca/dragon/salmonella.htm> (14 November 2002).

2. Secondary Web Page

A secondary Web page is part of a larger Web project. The page has a title but also features the name of the project as well.

Endnote/Footnote:

> 14. Trudy Kuhrt, "Trachemys Scripta," *Animal Diversity Web,* 2 May 2001,
>
> <http://animaldiversity.ummz.umich.edu/accounts/trachemys/
>
> t._scripta$narrative.html> (14 November 2002).

Bibliography:

> Kuhrt, Trudy. "Trachemys Scripta." *Animal Diversity Web.* 2 May 2001.
>
> <http://animaldiversity.ummz.umich.edu/accounts/trachemys/
>
> t._scripta$narrative.html> (14 November 2002).

3. Online Journal Article

An online journal article is the electronic text of a previously printed article (now available on the Web) or a document available only on the Internet.

(When an article has appeared previously in print)
Endnote/Footnote:

> 15. C. Levy et al., "Reptile-Associated Salmonellosis—Selected States,
>
> 1996–1998," *Morbidity and Mortality Weekly Report* 48 (1999): 1009–13,
>
> <http://www.cdc.gov/epo/mmwrpreview/mmwrhtml/mm4844a1.htm>
>
> (14 November 2002).

Bibliography:

> Levy, C., M. Finnerty, G. Hansen, and B. Matyas. "Reptile-Associated
>
> Salmonellosis—Selected States, 1996–1998." *Morbidity and Mortality Weekly*
>
> *Report* 48 (1999): 1009–13. <http://www.cdc.gov/epo/mmwrpreview/
>
> mmwrhtml/mm4844a1.htm> (14 November 2002).

(When an article has never been published in print, but appears only in an on___ publication)
Endnote/Footnote:

> 16. Elsie Rosner, "Salmonellosis from a Trip to the Zoo," *Physician's Weekly* 13, no. 39 (1996), <http://www.physweekly.com/archive/96/10_21_96/ cu4.html> (14 November 2002).

Bibliography:

> Rosner, Elsie. "Salmonellosis from a Trip to the Zoo." *Physician's Weekly* 13, no. 39 (1996). <http://www.physweekly.com/archive/96/10_21_96/ cu4.html> (14 November 2002).

4. Online Magazine Article

An online magazine article is the electronic text of a previously printed article (now available on the Web) or a document available only on the Internet.

(When an article has appeared previously in print)
Endnote/Footnote:

> 17. Michelle Pullia Turk, "New Food Rules for Pregnancy," *Parents,* July 2001: 32–3, <http://www.parents.com/articles/pregnancy/1186.jsp> (14 November 2002).

Bibliography:

> Turk, Michelle Pullia. "New Food Rules for Pregnancy." *Parents,* July 2001: 32–3. <http://www.parents.com/articles/pregnancy/1186.jsp> (14 November 2002).

(When an article has never been published in print, but appears only in an online publication)
Endnote/Footnote:

> 18. "Is Your Child Safe from Salmonella?" *Medscape Health for Consumers,* February 2000, <http://cbshealthwatch.aol.com/cx/viewarticle/210245> (14 November 2002).

Bibliography:

> "Is Your Child Safe from Salmonella?" *Medscape Health for Consumers,* February 2000. <http://cbshealthwatch.aol.com/cx/viewarticle/210245> (14 November 2002).

ine   *clopedia Article*

note:

. *Encyclopedia Britannica,* online ed., s.v. "salmonellosis," <http://
www.britannica.com/eb/article?eu=66794> (14 November 2002).

clopedia and dictionaries are not included in the bibliography.

5. *Online Government Publication*

Endnote/Footnote:

20. Utah, Department of Health, *Reptile-Associated Salmonellosis* (Salt Lake
City: Bureau of Epidemiology, 2001), <http://hlunix.hl.state.ut.us/els/
epidemiology/epifacts/reptile.html> (14 November 2002).

Bibliography:

Utah. Department of Health. *Reptile-Associated Salmonellosis.* Salt Lake City:
Bureau of Epidemiology, 2001. 13 December 2001.
<http://hlunix.hl.state.ut.us/els/epidemiology/epifacts/reptile.html>
(14 November 2002).

7. *Portion of an Online Book*

Endnote/Footnote:

21. F. Wayne King and Russell L. Burke, eds., "Checklist of Crocodilians,
Tuatara, and Turtles of the World," in *Crocodilian, Tuatara, and Turtle:
An Online Taxonomic and Geographic Reference* April 1997, <http://
www.flmnh. ufl.edu/natsci/herpetology/turtcroclist/chklst7.htm>
(11 December 2002).

Bibliography:

King, F. Wayne, and Russell L. Burke, eds. "Checklist of Crocodilians,
Tuatara, and Turtles." In *Crocodilian, Tuatara, and Turtle: An
Online Taxonomic and Geographic Reference.* 7 April 1997. <http://
www.flmnh.ufl.edu/natsci/herpetology/turtcroclist/chklst7.htm>
(11 December 2002).

8. Online Forum Posting

Endnote/Footnote:

> 22. Peteralbrian, "Treating parasites without fecals," 23 April 2003,
> <http://forum.kingsnake.com/health/messages/5960.html>
> (7 July 2003).

Bibliography:

> Peteralbrian. "Treating parasites without fecals." 23 April 2003.
> <http://forum.kingsnake.com/health/messages/5960.html>
> (7 July 2003).

Electronic Documents with Restricted Access. These entries usually do not include a URL because they require a subscription, password, or CD-ROM to access them. Cite as much of the required information as you can reasonably obtain.

1. Articles from a Database

Journal Article from a Database:
Endnote/Footnote:

> 23. Carol Lewis, "The Fright of the Iguana," *FDA Consumer* 31, no. 7 (1997):
> 35. *Academic Search Premier Database,* EBSCOhost (15 November 2002).

Bibliography:

> Lewis, Carol. "The Fright of the Iguana." *FDA Consumer* 31, no. 7 (1997):
> 33–36. *Academic Search Premier Database.* EBSCOhost (15 November 2002).

Magazine Article from a Database:
Endnote/Footnote:

> 24. Chris W. Lecos, "Risky Shell Game: Pet Turtles Can Infect Kids," *FDA Consumer* December–January 1987: 19. *InfoTrac College Edition,* Gale Group (15 November 2002).

Bibliography:

> Lecos, Chris W. "Risky Shell Game: Pet Turtles Can Infect Kids." *FDA Consumer* December–January 1987: 19–21. *InfoTrac College Edition,* Gale Group. (15 November 2002).

⊙ *Quick* CHECK

CMS Articles in a Database Format
Articles from a database should include the following information.

- Author's or editor's name
- Title of article in quotation marks
- Title of periodical, in italics
- Volume and issue numbers (if relevant)
- Date of publication (in parentheses)
- Page number(s)
- Title of database, in italics
- Name of service
- Date of access, in parentheses

---

2. Encyclopedia Article from a CD-ROM
Endnote/Footnote:

> 25. *Compton's Interactive Encyclopedia,* CD-ROM Version, 2000Dlx., s.v. "salmonella."

Encyclopedia and dictionaries are not included in the bibliography.

3. E-Mail Message
Include the author's name, subject line in quotation marks, date of sending, type of communication (personal e-mail, distribution list, office communication), and date of access, in parentheses.
Endnote/Footnote:

> 26. Janice Peppers, "Salmonellosis in Turtles," 10 May 2002, personal e-mail,
>
> (12 May 2002).

Bibliography:

> Peppers, Janice. "Salmonellosis in Turtles." 10 May 2002. Personal e-mail.
>
> (12 May 2002).

Index